# WAR & CONFLICT

### EDITED BY BENJAMIN HULME-CROSS

**OXFORD**
UNIVERSITY PRESS

# OXFORD
UNIVERSITY PRESS

Great Clarendon Street, Oxford, OX2 6DP, United Kingdom

Oxford University Press is a department of the University of Oxford.
It furthers the University's objective of excellence in research, scholarship,
and education by publishing worldwide. Oxford is a registered trade mark of Oxford
University Press in the UK and in certain other countries

This selection and arrangement © Benjamin Hulme-Cross 2013

The moral rights of the author have been asserted

First published in 2014

This educational edition published in 2021.

All rights reserved. No part of this publication may be reproduced, stored in a retrieval system, or transmitted, in any form or by any means, without the prior permission in writing of Oxford University Press, or as expressly permitted by law, by licence or under terms agreed with the appropriate reprographics rights organization. Enquiries concerning reproduction outside the scope of the above should be sent to the Rights Department, Oxford University Press, at the address above.

You must not circulate this work in any other form
and you must impose this same condition on any acquirer

British Library Cataloguing in Publication Data
Data available

978-1-3820-2870-7

1 3 5 7 9 10 8 6 4 2

Printed in Great Britain by CPI Group (UK) Ltd., Croydon CR0 4YY

## Acknowledgements

The author and publisher are grateful to the following for permission
to reproduce copyright material:
p2 Matt Whyman 'Eclipsed' copyright © Matt Whyman 2010, granted by LAW Agency; p37 Susan Gates 'No Man's Land' copyright © Susan Gates 2002, granted by David Higham Associates Ltd; p51 Robert Graves 'Christmas Truce' © Robert Graves 1962, granted by Carcanet Press Ltd; p72 Robert Westall 'Zakky' © copyright Estate of Robert Westall 1995; p96 Graham Greene 'The Destructors', from *Twenty-One Stories* © Graham Greene 1975, granted by David Higham Associates Ltd; p116 Geraldine McCaughrean 'Ex voto' copyright © Geraldine McCaughrean 2005, granted by David Higham Associates Ltd; p133 Jamila Gavin 'The Princess Spy' copyright © Jamila Gavin 2005, granted by David Higham Associates Ltd; p165 Eva Ibbotson: 'A Place on the Piano', copyright © The Estate of Eva Ibbotson, first published in *Brave New Words* edited by Sam Custance (Heinemann, 2008), used by permission of Curtis Brown Group Ltd, London; p200 John Agard 'In Times of Peace', copyright © Guardian News & Media Ltd 2009.

We have made every effort to trace and contact all copyright holders before publication. If notified, the publisher will rectify any errors or omissions at the earliest opportunity.

# Contents

**Stories**

| | |
|---|---|
| **Introduction** | **1** |
| 'Eclipsed', Matt Whyman | 2 |
| 'The Land Ironclads', H.G. Wells | 11 |
| **Introduction** | **49** |
| 'No Man's Land', Susan Gates | 50 |
| 'Christmas Truce', Robert Graves | 68 |
| **Introduction** | **97** |
| 'Zakky', Robert Westall | 98 |
| 'The Destructors', Graham Greene | 131 |
| **Introduction** | **157** |
| 'Ex Voto', Geraldine McCaughrean | 158 |
| 'The War Prayer', Mark Twain | 174 |
| **Introduction** | **180** |
| 'The Princess Spy', Jamila Gavin | 181 |
| 'His Last Bow', Arthur Conan Doyle | 195 |
| **Introduction** | **222** |
| 'A Place on the Piano', Eva Ibbotson | 223 |
| 'Swept and Garnished', Rudyard Kipling | 242 |

**Poems**
'The Charge of the Light Brigade', Alfred Lord Tennyson 256
'Dulce et Decorum Est', Wilfred Owen 260
'Tommy', Rudyard Kipling 263
'In Times of Peace', John Agard 268

# INTRODUCTION

'Eclipsed', Matt Whyman
'The Land Ironclads', H.G. Wells

Most war stories deal in harsh realities. However, some are wildly imaginative. H.G. Wells wrote 'The Land Ironclads' as a work of science fiction at the end of the nineteenth century and through it created a harsh reality of his own. Two decades later, Winston Churchill wrote to the author during the First World War, thanking him for providing the idea that formed the basis of the tank.

We must all hope that Matt Whyman's story is not so prophetic, set as it is against the backdrop of a world in turmoil after the moon has been blown up by a missile.

An interesting comparison could be made between these two stories by looking at how the individual experiences of characters and the theme of war are used to reveal more about each other.

# ECLIPSED

## Matt Whyman

I missed the moment that the moon exploded. Like so many people, I was fast asleep when it happened. According to my friend Maisie, whose neighbour works a night shift, it looked just like a mothball fragmenting into the void.

The morning after, I discovered my father staring out of the kitchen window. He was barely blinking. On the radio a news report claimed that America was demanding some explanation from the Soviets. At a time when the world lived in fear of a nuclear strike from one side or the other, it seemed like an act of madness for Russia to launch a lunar attack. My father didn't appear to be listening, however, and at first I didn't realize the enormity of what was being broadcast. It was only when I sneezed on account of my hay fever that he noticed me.

'Sleep well, cupcake?' he asked.

'Sure,' I told him, looking around. 'Where's Mum?'

As he pressed his lips into a smile, I noticed his eyes shine over. 'She'll be back later,' he said after a moment. 'I promised her I'd tell you that.'

At school I found everyone talking about the same thing. At first I thought I was the victim of a grand hoax. How could the moon just cease to exist? I had only been alive for fourteen years. Considering a lifetime without it seemed unthinkable. I remember that first day was clear and bright. The sky, as blue as a lagoon, had not a cloud in sight. During a special assembly, our headmistress explained that with the loss of the moon we faced a time of great uncertainty. Nobody knew for sure what effect its disappearance would have on everything, from the ebb and flow of the oceans' tides to the rate at which the earth revolved. Still, she assured us that nature would adapt and survive, as would mankind.

Throughout each lesson that followed, we kept turning our attention to the window. Even the teachers couldn't resist looking, despite the fact that there was nothing unusual to see.

Come dusk, as we made our way to our homes, stars began to prick the twilight. I kept looking up and around. I wasn't sure what I was hoping to spot. The moon might have sailed through every night sky for billions of years, but sometimes clouds, tall buildings or trees conspired to cover it up. Everything just looked so normal up there, so peaceful and serene. I saw no smouldering remains or hole torn out of the heavens. Had I spent the day in my own company, without news or gossip, it would not have struck me that anything was different. Still, as an urgent breeze picked up all the litter in the streets, I couldn't help feeling that perhaps we had taken things for granted.

'Come and sit with us, cupcake. There's something we need to discuss.'

I had found my parents facing one another at the kitchen table. Like everyone, they appeared a little shell-shocked and bewildered. They looked up when I came into the room. As soon as my father invited me to join them, I realized I had just killed a conversation.

'What's the latest on the moon?' I asked, noting the television switched on in the corner. The sound was muted, but the footage of the rockets climbing into the sky looked ominous.

'The moon?' My father paused and gazed at me. It left me feeling like I hadn't returned home in years. 'I'm not sure,' he said, and cleared his throat. 'What did they tell you at school?'

I drew a chair from the table and sat with them. 'The

Russians are claiming a test firing went badly wrong. That's what our form teacher told us before the bell rang. They're suggesting the target coordinates were changed as an act of sabotage by the United States.'

Mum clasped her mug with both hands. Not once did she take her eyes off it. 'The last time I looked at the moon,' she said, 'it was on the wane.'

I glanced at Dad, confused by her comment. 'Mum,' I said, 'it isn't coming back.'

Outside, the wind had strengthened so much that it began to moan and whistle. Only then did I notice that the curtains had been closed against the night sky. I looked at my dad, and found his focus upon me once again.

'This isn't about the moon,' he said. 'It's about us.'

Until they told me Mum was moving out, I really hadn't known that my parents had been having problems. As it turned out, I don't think my dad had either. Sure, Mum would sometimes say that he loved his work more than he loved us, but we'd never taken her seriously. Looking back, I suppose this was her way of quietly convincing herself that the changes in her heart were for the best. I didn't cry when Mum revealed that she'd met someone else. I just nodded when she promised me that everything would be OK, and stared at the table when Dad began to weep.

'I should go,' my mother said. 'I would ask you to come with me, Lottie, but space is an issue and this is only for the very short term. Your father and I have a lot of sorting out to do, but we've agreed that you come first. Once we sell this house, we'll have enough money to provide you with two places you can call home.'

'But I don't want to move,' I said. 'And I don't want you to go.'

My mother rose from the table. She circled behind my father, touched his shoulder for a moment and then headed for the door. When she opened it, the howling I could hear out there sounded like another world entirely.

The first few nights were the worst. I suppose we had to get used to the loss and what it meant for us all. The winds struck at sunset and only calmed as dawn broke. In the darkest hours gusts would rampage across town and country with such violence that I couldn't sleep. The experts explained how this was due to the absence of a gravitational pull. As I looked at the impact around me, it seemed more like the loss of a calming influence.

On the television Dad and I watched endless news footage of tidal surges and oceanic whirlpools. It looked to me like God had got fed up with us all and decided to pull the plug. All my favourite programmes were replaced by reports about emerging changes to our planet. Birds flocked in unusual directions, clouds formed strange new shapes, and dogs howled after midnight as if plagued by a frequency beyond our hearing.

Even people behaved differently. Many panicked, with riots taking place as far afield as Reykjavik, Moscow and Rio de Janeiro. I also heard from Maisie that her neighbour had switched to a day shift on account of all the late night looting. As for me, I found my hay fever disappeared completely.

At home our cat reacted badly to the situation. It didn't help that Mum was the one who had always taken care of him. After she left he went hungry for several days because Dad and I completely forgot to feed him. Worse still, the high winds really spooked the poor thing. Instead of spending his nights out on the prowl, he chose to stay indoors. Even with the calm that came at daybreak, he would pop out only for a very short time. Then he'd crash back through the cat flap as if chased in by a snarling dog.

"What's frightening him?' I asked on one occasion.

My father considered this for a moment, watching the fur on the cat's back settle. 'Change,' he said finally. 'It's an unsettling time for us all.'

Throughout this period, while most governments appealed for calm, the two superpowers continued to raise the temperature. In an address to the world President Reagan not only denied all involvement in the moon strike, but even went so far as to suggest that the Russians had been attempting a surprise attack on American defence satellites. One which had ended in a cosmic disaster for us all. As each side had primed their nuclear arsenal to take flight, I asked if we should prepare a fallout shelter. In response, Dad turned to me as if emerging from a dream, and said it was too late for that.

\*\*\*

I was at school when Mum first returned to pick up some things. I knew she had been here as soon as I walked in. Her perfume hung in the air and the cat was at his bowl, finishing a treat of canned tuna.

Then, late last night, she came back again. I was in bed when I heard the key in the lock. Normally at that hour I'd have been asleep but, what with the high winds, I was wide awake.

I heard her close the door against the gale, and then her voice calling softly for my father. I wanted to get up and see her. I really did. I was just worried that by padding downstairs, somehow I would scare her away. A moment later, my parents were speaking in the kitchen.

It struck me then that Dad hadn't shown any anger about the situation. He wasn't like the president, whose emotions were quite clear each time he made a broadcast. Reagan didn't shout or beat the desk with his fist, but you could see it in his face. From a tension in his jawline to the way his eyes pinched when he outlined the American position. My dad didn't carry that kind of fire within him. Once he had stopped weeping, there was nothing left.

As I listened to them from my bed, it sounded as if my mother was doing all the talking. At one point I even heard some words.

'I'm sorry,' she said. *'I'm just sorry'.*

\*\*\*

The storm that night was more ferocious than anything we had experienced. It raged so hard against my window that I was too scared to climb out and peek through the curtains. I just pulled my duvet over my head, and prayed the house would not be blown to bits.

Now, as sunrise sees the winds subside, I look out and catch my breath. Trees have come down everywhere, bringing power lines with them, while somewhere in the distance I can hear a voice droning through a megaphone. Weirdly, though, the street is deserted. I switch on my radio, if only for some company, and that's when I hear about the emergency measures.

*'Dad!'*

Grabbing my dressing-gown, I rush across the landing to the main bedroom. If the government really have ordered troops onto the street, there'll be no school today for sure. I don't pause to knock. I throw open the door and then stop in my tracks.

I'm surprised to find the cat curled up at the foot of the bed. My father is sound asleep, but what leaves me reeling is the sight of the woman in his arms. Her head is resting upon his shoulder, with her palm flat on his chest. She opens her eyes and looks at me. At first, we just gaze at one another.

'We've been ordered to stay inside,' I say eventually, blinking back tears. 'It's chaos out there.'

Just then, from somewhere over the hills, we hear the crack of gunfire. The sound takes a moment to decay, as if refusing to fall silent.

'Things will never be the same again,' says Mum in barely a whisper. 'All we can do is hope that we're over the worst.'

# THE LAND IRONCLADS

## H.G. Wells

### I

The young lieutenant lay beside the war correspondent and admired the idyllic calm of the enemy's lines through his field-glass.

'So far as I can see,' he said, at last, 'one man.'

'What's he doing?' asked the war correspondent.

'Field-glass at us,' said the young lieutenant

'And this is war!'

'No,' said the young lieutenant; 'it's Bloch.'

'The game's a draw.'

'No! They've got to win or else they lose. A draw's a win for our side.'

They had discussed the political situation fifty times or so, and the war correspondent was weary of it. He stretched out his limbs. 'Aaai s'pose it *is*!' he yawned.

'*Flut!*'

'What was that?'

'Shot at us.'

The war correspondent shifted to a slightly lower position. 'No one shot at him,' he complained.

'I wonder if they think we shall get so bored we shall go home?'

The war correspondent made no reply.

'There's the harvest, of course. ...'

They had been there a month. Since the first brisk movements after the declaration of war things had gone slower and slower, until it seemed as though the whole machine of events must have run down. To begin with, they had had almost a scampering time; the invader had come across the frontier on the very dawn of the war in half-a-dozen parallel columns behind a cloud of cyclists and cavalry, with a general air of coming straight on the capital, and the defender horsemen had held him up, and peppered him and forced him to open out to outflank, and had then bolted to the next position in the most approved style, for a couple of days, until in the afternoon, bump! they had the invader against their prepared lines of defence. He did not suffer so much as had been hoped and expected: he was coming on, it seemed with his eyes open, his scouts winded the guns, and down he sat at once without the shadow of an attack and began grubbing trenches for himself, as though he meant to sit down there to the very end of time. He was slow, but much more wary than the world had been led to expect, and he kept convoys tucked in and shielded his slow marching infantry sufficiently well to prevent any heavy adverse scoring.

'But he ought to attack,' the young lieutenant had insisted.

'He'll attack us at dawn, somewhere along the lines. You'll get the bayonets coming into the trenches just about when you can see,' the war correspondent had held until a week ago.

The young lieutenant winked when he said that.

When one early morning the men the defenders sent to lie out five hundred yards before the trenches, with a view to the unexpected emptying of magazines into any night attack, gave way to causeless panic and blazed away at nothing for ten minutes, the war correspondent understood the meaning of that wink.

'What would you do if you were the enemy?' said the war correspondent, suddenly.

'If I had men like I've got now?'

'Yes.'

'Take those trenches.'

'How?'

'Oh – dodges! Crawl out half-way at night before moonrise and get into touch with the chaps we send out. Blaze at 'em if they tried to shift, and so bag some of 'em in the daylight. Learn that patch of ground by heart, lie all day in squatty holes, and come on nearer next night. There's a bit over there, lumpy ground, where they could get across to rushing distance – easy. In a night or so. It would be a mere game for our fellows; it's what they're made for. ... Guns? Shrapnel and stuff wouldn't stop good men who meant business.'

'Why don't *they* do that?'

'Their men aren't brutes enough: that's the trouble. They're a crowd of devitalised townsmen, and that's the truth of the matter. They're clerks, they're factory hands, they're students, they're civilised men. They can write, they can talk, they can make and do all sorts of things, but they're poor amateurs at war. They've got no physical staying power, and that's the whole thing. They've never slept in the open one night in their lives; they've never drunk anything but the purest water-company water; they've never gone short of three meals a day since they left their feeding-bottles. Half their cavalry never cocked leg over horse till it enlisted six months ago. They ride their horses as though they were bicycles – you watch 'em! They're fools at the game, and they know it. Our boys of fourteen can give their grown men points. ... Very well –'

The war correspondent mused on his face with his nose between his knuckles.

'If a decent civilisation,' he said, 'cannot produce better men for war than –'

He stopped with belated politeness.

'I mean –'

'Than our open-air life,' said the young lieutenant, politely.

'Exactly,' said the war correspondent. 'Then civilisation has to stop.'

'It looks like it,' the young lieutenant admitted.

'Civilisation has science, you know,' said the war correspondent. 'It invented and it makes the rifles and guns and things you use.'

'Which our nice healthy hunters and stockmen and so on, rowdy-dowdy cowpunchers and negro-whackers, can use ten times better than – *What's that?*'

'What?' said the war correspondent, and then seeing his companion busy with his field-glass he produced his own: 'Where?' said the war correspondent, sweeping the enemy's lines.

'It's nothing' said the young lieutenant, still looking.

'What's nothing?'

The young lieutenant put down his glass and pointed. 'I thought I saw something there, behind the stems of those trees. Something black. What it was I don't know.'

The war correspondent tried to get even by intense scrutiny.

'It wasn't anything' said the young lieutenant,

rolling over to regard the darkling evening sky, and generalised: 'There never will be anything any more for ever. Unless –'

The war correspondent looked inquiry.

'They may get their stomachs wrong, or something – living without proper drains.'

A sound of bugles came from the tents behind. The war correspondent slid backward down the sand and stood up. 'Boom!' came from somewhere far away to the left. 'Halloa!' he said, hesitated, and crawled back to peer again. 'Firing at this time is jolly bad manners.'

The young lieutenant was incommunicative again for a space.

Then he pointed to the distant clump of trees again. 'One of our big guns. They were firing at that,' he said.

'The thing that wasn't anything?'

'Something over there, anyhow.'

Both men were silent, peering through their glasses for a space. 'Just when it's twilight,' the lieutenant complained. He stood up.

'I might stay here a bit,' said the war correspondent.

The lieutenant shook his head. 'There is nothing to see,' he apologised, and then went down to where his little squad of sun-brown, loose-limbed men had been yarning in the trench. The war correspondent stood up also, glanced for a moment at the business-like bustle below him, gave perhaps twenty seconds to those enigmatical trees again, then turned his face toward the camp.

He found himself wondering whether his editor would consider the story of how somebody thought he saw something black behind a clump of trees, and how a gun was fired at this illusion by somebody else, too trivial for public consultation.

'It's the only gleam of a shadow of interest,' said the war correspondent, 'for ten whole days.'

'No,' he said, presently; 'I'll write that other article, "Is War Played Out?"'

He surveyed the darkling lines in perspective, the tangle of trenches one behind another, one commanding another, which the defender had made ready. The shadows and mists swallowed up their receding contours, and here and there a lantern gleamed, and here and there knots of men were busy about small fires.

'No troops on earth could do it,' he said. ...

He was depressed. He believed that there were other things in life better worth having than proficiency in war; he believed that in the heart of civilisation, for all its stresses, its crushing concentrations of forces, its injustice and suffering, there lay something that might be the hope of the world, and the idea that any people by living in the open air, hunting perpetually, losing touch with books and art and all the things that intensify life, might hope to resist and break that great development to the end of time, jarred on his civilised soul.

Apt to his thought came a file of defender soldiers and passed him in the gleam of a swinging lamp that marked the way.

He glanced at their red-lit faces, and one shone out for a moment, a common type of face in the defender's ranks: ill-shaped nose, sensuous lips, bright clear eyes full of alert cunning, slouch hat cocked on one side and adorned with the peacock's plume of the rustic Don Juan turned soldier, a hard brown skin, a sinewy frame, an open, tireless stride, and a master's grip on the rifle.

The war correspondent returned their salutations and went on his way.

'Louts,' he whispered. 'Cunning, elementary louts. And they are going to beat the townsmen at the game of war!'

From the red glow among the nearer tents came first one and then half-a-dozen hearty voices, bawling in a drawling unison the words of a particularly slab and sentimental patriotic song.

'Oh, *go* it!' muttered the war correspondent, bitterly.

## II

It was opposite the trenches called after Hackbone's Hut that the battle began. There the ground stretched broad and level between the lines, with scarcely shelter for a lizard, and it seemed to the startled, just awakened men who came crowding into the trenches that this was one more proof of that green inexperience of the enemy of which they had heard so much. The war correspondent would not believe his ears at first, and swore that he and the war artist, who, still imperfectly roused, was trying to put on his boots by the light of a match held in his hand, were the victims of a common illusion. Then, after putting his head in a bucket of cold water, his intelligence came back as he towelled. He listened. 'Gollys!' he said; 'that's something more than scare firing this time. It's like ten thousand carts on a bridge of tin.'

There came a sort of enrichment to that steady uproar. 'Machine-guns!'

Then, 'Guns!'

The artist, with one boot on, thought to look at his watch, and went to it hopping.

'Half an hour from dawn,' he said. 'You were right about their attacking, after all. ...'

The war correspondent came out of the tent, verifying the presence of chocolate in his pocket as he did so. He had to halt for a moment or so until his eyes were toned down to the night a little. 'Pitch!' he said. He stood for a space to season his eyes before he felt justified in striking out for a black gap among the adjacent tents. The artist coming out behind him fell over a tent-rope. It was half-past two o'clock in the morning of the darkest night in time, and against a sky of dull black silk the enemy was talking searchlights, a wild jabber of searchlights. 'He's trying to blind our riflemen,' said the war correspondent with a flash, and waited for the artist and then set off with a sort of discreet haste again. 'Whoa!' he said, presently. 'Ditches!'

They stopped.

'It's the confounded searchlights,' said the war correspondent.

They saw lanterns going to and fro, nearby, and men falling in to march down to the trenches. They were for following them, and then the artist began to feel his night eyes. 'If we scramble this,' he said, 'and it's only a drain, there's a clear run up to the ridge.' And that way they took. Lights came and went in the tents behind, as the men turned out, and ever and again they came to broken ground and staggered and stumbled. But in a little while they drew near the crest. Something that sounded like the impact of a very important railway accident happened in the air above them, and the shrapnel bullets seethed about them like a sudden handful of hail. 'Right-ho!' said the war correspondent, and soon they judged they had come to the crest and stood in the midst of a world of great darkness and frantic glares, whose principal fact was sound.

Right and left of them and all about them was the uproar, an army-full of magazine fire, at first chaotic and monstrous and then, eked out by little flashes and gleams and suggestions, taking the beginnings of a shape. It looked to the war correspondent as though the enemy must have attacked in line and with his whole force – in which case he was either being or was already annihilated.

'Dawn and the dead,' he said, with his instinct for headlines. He said this to himself, but afterwards, by means of shouting, he conveyed an idea to the artist.

'They must have meant it for a surprise,' he said.

It was remarkable how the firing kept on. After a time he began to perceive a sort of rhythm in this inferno of noise. It would decline – decline perceptibly, droop towards something that was comparatively a pause – a pause of inquiry. 'Aren't you all dead yet?' this pause seemed to say. The flickering fringe of rifle-flashes would become attenuated and broken, and the whack-bang of the enemy's big guns two miles away there would come up out of the deeps. Then suddenly, east or west of them, something would startle the rifles to a frantic outbreak again.

The war correspondent taxed his brain for some theory of conflict that would account for this, and was suddenly aware that the artist and he were vividly illuminated. He could see the ridge on which they stood and before them in black outline a file of riflemen hurrying down towards the nearer trenches. It became visible that a light rain was falling, and farther away towards the enemy was a clear space with men – 'our men?' – running across it in disorder. He saw one of those men throw up his hands and drop. And something else black and shining loomed up on the edge of the beam-coruscating flashes; and behind it and far away a calm, white eye regarded the world. 'Whit, whit, whit,' sang something in the air, and then the artist was running for cover, with the war correspondent behind him. Bang came shrapnel, bursting close at hand as it seemed, and our two men were lying flat in a dip in the ground, and the light and everything had gone again, leaving a vast note of interrogation upon the night.

The war correspondent came within bawling range. 'What the deuce was it? Shooting our men down!'

'Black,' said the artist, 'and like a fort. Not two hundred yards from the first trench.'

He sought for comparisons in his mind. 'Something

between a big blockhouse and a giant's dish-cover,' he said.

'And they were running!' said the war correspondent.

'*You'd* run if a thing like that, searchlight to help it, turned up like a prowling nightmare in the middle of the night.'

They crawled to what they judged the edge of the dip and lay regarding the unfathomable dark. For a space they could distinguish nothing, and then a sudden convergence of the searchlights of both sides brought the strange thing out again.

In that flickering pallor it had the effect of a large and clumsy black insect, an insect the size of an ironclad cruiser, crawling obliquely to the first line of trenches and firing shots out of portholes in its side. And on its carcass the bullets must have been battering with more than the passionate violence of hail on a roof of tin.

Then in the twinkling of an eye the curtain of the dark had fallen again and the monster had vanished, but the crescendo of musketry marked its approach to the trenches.

They were beginning to talk about the thing to each other, when a flying bullet kicked dirt into the artist's face, and they decided abruptly to crawl down into the cover of the trenches. They had got down with an unobtrusive persistence into the second line, before the dawn had grown clear enough for anything to be seen. They found themselves in a crowd of expectant riflemen, all noisily arguing about what would happen next. The enemy's contrivance had done execution upon the outlying men, it seemed, but they did not believe it would do any more. 'Come the day and we'll capture the lot of them,' said a burly soldier.

'Them?' said the war correspondent.

'They say there's a regular string of 'em, crawling along the front of our lines. ... Who cares?'

The darkness filtered away so imperceptibly that at no moment could one declare decisively that one could see. The searchlights ceased to sweep hither and thither. The enemy's monsters were dubious patches of darkness upon the dark, and then no longer dubious, and so they crept out into distinctness. The war correspondent, munching chocolate absent-mindedly, beheld at last a spacious picture of battle under the cheerless sky, whose central focus was an array of fourteen or fifteen huge clumsy shapes lying in perspective on the very edge of the first line of trenches, at intervals of perhaps three hundred yards, and evidently firing down upon the crowded riflemen. They were so close in that the defender's guns had ceased, and only the first line of trenches was in action.

The second line commanded the first, and as the

light grew the war correspondent could make out the riflemen who were fighting these monsters, crouched in knots and crowds behind the transverse banks that crossed the trenches against the eventuality of an enfilade. The trenches close to the big machines were empty save for the crumpled suggestions of dead and wounded men; the defenders had been driven right and left as soon as the prow of this land ironclad had loomed up over the front of the trench. He produced his field-glass, and was immediately a centre of inquiry from the soldiers about him.

They wanted to look, they asked questions, and after he had announced that the men across the traverses seemed unable to advance or retreat, and were crouching under cover rather than fighting, he found it advisable to loan his glasses to a burly and incredulous corporal. He heard a strident voice, and found a lean and sallow soldier at his back talking to the artist.

'There's chaps down there caught,' the man was saying. 'If they retreat they got to expose themselves, and the fire's too straight. –'

'They aren't firing much, but every shot's a hit.'

'Who?'

'The chaps in that thing. The men who're coming up –'

'Coming up where?'

'We're evacuating them trenches where we can. Our chaps are coming back up the zigzags. ... No end of 'em hit. ... But when we get clear our turn'll come. Rather! These things won't be able to cross a trench or get into it; and before they can get back our guns'll smash 'em up. Smash 'em right up. See?' A brightness came into his eyes. 'Then we'll have a go at the beggar inside,' he said. ...

The war correspondent thought for a moment, trying to realise the idea. Then he set himself to recover his field-glasses from the burly corporal. ...

The daylight was getting clearer now. The clouds were lifting, and a gleam of lemon-yellow amidst the level masses to the east portended sunrise. He looked again at the land ironclad. As he saw it in the bleak grey dawn, lying obliquely upon the slope and on the very lip of the foremost trench, the suggestion of a stranded vessel was very great indeed. It might have been from eighty to a hundred feet long – it was about two hundred and fifty yards away – its vertical side was ten feet high or so, smooth for that height, and then with a complex patterning under the eaves of its flattish turtle cover. This patterning was a close interlacing of portholes, rifle barrels, and telescope tubes – sham and real – indistinguishable one from the other. The thing had come into such a position as to enfilade the trench, which was empty now, so far as he could see, except for two or three crouching knots of men and the tumbled dead. Behind it, across the plain, it had scored the grass with a train of linked impressions, like the dotted tracings sea-things leave in sand. Left and right of that track dead men and wounded men were scattered – men it had picked off as they fled back from their advanced positions in the searchlight glare from the invader's lines. And now it lay with its head projecting a little over the trench it had won, as if it were a single sentient thing planning the next phase of its attack. ...

He lowered his glasses and took a more comprehensive view of the situation. These creatures of the night had evidently won the first line of trenches and the fight had come to a pause. In the increasing light he could make out by a stray shot or a chance exposure that the defender's marksmen were lying thick in the second and third line of trenches up towards the low crest of the position, and in such of the zigzags as gave them a chance of a converging fire. The men about him were talking of guns. 'We're in the line of the big guns at the crest but they'll soon shift one to pepper them,' the lean man said, reassuringly.

'Whup,' said the corporal.

'Bang! bang! bang! Whir-r-r-r-r!' It was a sort of nervous jump, and all the rifles were going off by themselves. The war correspondent found himself and the artist, two idle men crouching behind a line of preoccupied backs, of industrious men discharging magazines. The monster had moved. It continued to move regardless of the hail that splashed its skin with bright new specks of lead. It was singing a mechanical little ditty to itself, 'Tuf-tuf, tuf-tuf, tuf-tuf,' and squirting out little jets of steam behind. It had humped itself up, as a limpet does before it crawls; it had lifted its skirt and displayed along the length of it – *feet*! They were thick, stumpy feet, between knobs and buttons in shape – flat, broad things, reminding one of the feet of elephants or the legs of caterpillars; and then, as the skirt rose higher, the war correspondent, scrutinising the thing through his glasses again, saw that these feet hung, as it were, on the rims of wheels. His thoughts whirled back to Victoria Street, Westminster, and he saw himself in the piping times of peace, seeking matter for an interview.

'Mr. – Mr. Diplock,' he said; 'and he called them Pedrails ... Fancy meeting them here!'

The marksman beside him raised his head and shoulders in a speculative mood to fire more certainly – it seemed so natural to assume the attention of the monster must be distracted by this trench before it – and was suddenly knocked backwards by a bullet through his neck. His feet flew up, and he vanished out of the margin of the watcher's field of vision.

The war correspondent grovelled tighter, but after a glance behind him at a painful little confusion, he resumed his field-glass, for the thing was putting down its feet one after the other, and hoisting itself farther and farther over the trench. Only a bullet in the head could have stopped him looking just then.

The lean man with the strident voice ceased firing to turn and reiterate his point. 'They can't possibly cross,' he bawled. 'They – '

'Bang! Bang! Bang! Bang!' – drowned everything.

The lean man continued speaking for a word or so, then gave it up, shook his head to enforce the impossibility of anything crossing a trench like the one below, and resumed business once more.

And all the while that great bulk was crossing. When the war correspondent turned his glass on it again it had bridged the trench, and its queer feet were rasping away at the farther bank, in the attempt to get a hold there. It got its hold. It continued to crawl until the greater bulk of it was over the trench – until it was all over. Then it paused for a moment, adjusted its skirt a little nearer the ground, gave an unnerving 'toot, toot,' and came on abruptly at a pace of, perhaps, six miles an hour straight up the gentle slope towards our observer.

The war correspondent raised himself on his elbow and looked a natural inquiry at the artist.

For a moment the men about him stuck to their position and fired furiously. Then the lean man in a mood of precipitancy slid backwards, and the war correspondent said 'Come along' to the artist, and led the movement along the trench.

As they dropped down, the vision of a hillside of trench being rushed by a dozen vast cockroaches disappeared for a space, and instead was one of a narrow passage, crowded with men, for the most part receding, though one or two turned or halted. He never turned back to see the nose of the monster creep over the brow of the trench; he never even troubled to keep in touch with the artist. He heard the 'whit' of bullets about him soon enough, and saw a man before him stumble and drop, and then he was one of a furious crowd fighting to get into a transverse zigzag ditch that enabled the defenders to get under cover up and down the hill. It was like a theatre panic. He gathered from signs and fragmentary words that on ahead another of these monsters had also won to the second trench.

He lost his interest in the general course of the battle for a space altogether; he became simply a modest egotist, in a mood of hasty circumspection, seeking the farthest rear, amidst a dispersed multitude of disconcerted riflemen similarly employed. He scrambled down through trenches, he took his courage in both hands and sprinted across the open, he had moments of panic when it seemed madness not to be quadrupedal, and moments of shame when he stood up and faced about to see how the fight was going. And he was one of many thousand very similar men that morning. On the ridge he halted in a knot of scrub, and was for a few minutes almost minded to stop and see things out.

The day was now fully come. The grey sky had changed to blue, and of all the cloudy masses of the dawn there remained only a few patches of dissolving fleeciness. The world below was bright and singularly clear. The ridge was not, perhaps, more than a hundred feet or so above the general plain, but in this flat region it sufficed to give the effect of extensive view. Away on the north side of the ridge, little and far, were the camps, the ordered wagons, all the gear of a big army; with officers galloping about and men doing aimless things. Here and there men were falling in, however, and the cavalry was forming up on the plain beyond the tents. The bulk of men who had been in the trenches were still on the move to the rear, scattered like sheep without a shepherd over the farther slopes. Here and there were little rallies and attempts to wait and do – something vague; but the general drift was away from any concentration. There on the southern side was the elaborate lacework of trenches and defences, across which these iron turtles, fourteen of them spread out over a line of perhaps three miles, were now advancing as fast as a man could trot, and methodically shooting down and breaking up any persistent knots of resistance. Here and there stood little clumps of men, outflanked and unable to get away, showing the white flag, and the invader's cyclist-infantry was advancing now across the open, in open order but unmolested, to complete the work of the machines. Surveyed at large, the defenders already looked a beaten army. A mechanism that was effectually ironclad against bullets, that could at a pinch cross a thirty-foot trench, and that seemed able to shoot out rifle-bullets with unerring precision, was clearly an inevitable victor against anything but rivers, precipices, and guns.

He looked at his watch. 'Half-past four! Lord! What things can happen in two hours. Here's the whole blessed army being walked over, and at half-past two –

'And even now our blessed louts haven't done a thing with their guns!'

He scanned the ridge right and left of him with his glasses. He turned again to the nearest land ironclad, advancing now obliquely to him and not three hundred yards away, and then scrambled the ground over which he must retreat if he was not to be captured.

'They'll do nothing,' he said, and glanced again at the enemy.

And then from far away to the left came the thud of a gun, followed very rapidly by a rolling gunfire.

He hesitated and decided to stay.

## III

The defender had relied chiefly upon his rifles in the event of an assault. His guns he kept concealed at various points upon and behind the ridge ready to bring them into action against any artillery preparations for an attack on the part of his antagonist. The situation had rushed upon him with the dawn, and by the time the gunners had their guns ready for motion, the land ironclads were already in among the foremost trenches. There is a natural reluctance to fire into one's own broken men, and many of the guns, being intended simply to fight an advance of the enemy's artillery, were not in positions to hit anything in the second line of trenches. After that the advance of the land ironclads was swift. The defender-general found himself suddenly called upon to invent a new sort of warfare, in which guns were to fight alone amidst broken and retreating infantry. He had scarcely thirty minutes in which to think it out. He did not respond to the call, and what happened that morning was that the advance of the land ironclads forced the fight, and each gun and battery made what play its circumstances dictated. For the most part it was poor play.

Some of the guns got in two or three shots, some one or two, and the percentage of misses was unusually high. The howitzers, of course, did nothing. The land ironclads in each case followed much the same tactics. As soon as a gun came into play the monster turned itself almost end on, so as to minimise the chances of a square hit, and made not for the gun, but for the nearest point on its flank from which the gunners could be shot down. Few of the hits scored were very effectual; only one of the things was disabled, and that was the one that fought the three batteries attached to the brigade on the left wing. Three that were hit when close upon the guns were clean shot through without being put out of action. Our war correspondent did not see that one momentary arrest of the tide of victory on the left; he saw only the very ineffectual fight of half-battery 96B close at hand upon his right. This he watched some time beyond the margin of safety.

Just after he heard the three batteries opening up upon his left he became aware of the thud of horses' hoofs from the sheltered side of the slope, and presently saw first one and then two other guns galloping into position along the north side of the ridge, well out of sight of the great bulk that was now creeping obliquely towards the crest and cutting up the lingering infantry beside it and below, as it came.

The half-battery swung round into line – each gun describing its curve – halted, unlimbered, and prepared for action. ...

'Bang!'

The land ironclad had become visible over the brow of the hill, and just visible as a long black back to the gunners. It halted, as though it hesitated.

The two remaining guns fired, and then their big antagonist had swung round and was in full view, end on, against the sky, coming at a rush.

The gunners became frantic in their haste to fire again. They were so near the war correspondent could see the expressions on their excited faces through his field-glass. As he looked he saw a man drop, and realised for the first time that the ironclad was shooting.

For a moment the big black monster crawled with an accelerated pace towards the furiously active gunners. Then, as if moved by a generous impulse, it turned its full broadside to their attack, and scarcely forty yards away from them. The war correspondent turned his field-glass back to the gunners and perceived it was now shooting down the men about the guns with the most deadly rapidity.

Just for a moment it seemed splendid and then it seemed horrible. The gunners were dropping in heaps about their guns. To lay a hand on a gun was death. 'Bang!' went the gun on the left, a hopeless miss, and that was the only second shot the half-battery fired. In another moment half-a-dozen surviving artillerymen were holding up their hands amidst a scattered muddle of dead and wounded men, and the fight was done.

The war correspondent hesitated between stopping in his scrub and waiting for an opportunity to surrender decently, or taking to an adjacent gully he had discovered. If he surrendered it was certain he would get no copy off; while, if he escaped, there were all sorts of chances. He decided to follow the gully, and take the first offer in the confusion beyond the camp of picking up a horse.

## IV

Subsequent authorities have found fault with the first land ironclads in many particulars, but assuredly they served their purpose on the day of their appearance. They were essentially long, narrow, and very strong steel frameworks carrying the engines, and borne upon eight pairs of big pedrail wheels, each about ten feet in diameter, each a driving wheel and set upon long axles free to swivel round a common axis. This arrangement gave them the maximum of adaptability to the contours of the ground. They crawled level along the ground with one foot high upon a hillock and another deep in a depression, and they could hold themselves erect and steady sideways upon even a steep hillside. The engineers directed the engines under the command of the captain, who had look-out points at small ports all round the upper edge of the adjustable skirt of twelve-inch iron-plating which protected the whole affair, and could also raise or depress a conning-tower set about the portholes through the centre of the iron top cover. The riflemen each occupied a small cabin of peculiar construction and these cabins were slung along the sides of and before and behind the great main framework, in a manner suggestive of the slinging of the seats of an Irish jaunting-car. Their rifles, however, were very different pieces of apparatus from the simple mechanisms in the hands of their adversaries.

These were in the first place automatic, ejected their cartridges and loaded again from a magazine each time they fired, until the ammunition store was at an end, and they had the most remarkable sights imaginable, sights which threw a bright little camera-obscura picture into the light-tight box in which the rifleman sat below. This camera-obscura picture was marked with two crossed lines, and whatever was covered by the intersection of these two lines, that the rifle hit. The sighting was ingeniously contrived. The rifleman stood at the table with a thing like an elaboration of a draughtsman's dividers in his hand, and he opened and closed these dividers, so that they were always at the apparent height – if it was an ordinary-sized man – of the man he wanted to kill. A little twisted strand of wire like an electric-light wire ran from this implement up to the gun, and as the dividers opened and shut the sights went up and down. Changes in the clearness of the atmosphere, due to changes of moisture, were met by an ingenious use of that meteorologically sensitive substance, catgut, and when the land ironclad moved forward the sites got a compensatory deflection in the direction of its motion. The riflemen stood up in his pitch-dark chamber and watched the little picture before him. One hand held the dividers for judging distance, and the other grasped a big knob like a door-handle. As he pushed this knob about the rifle above swung to correspond, and the picture passed to and fro like an agitated panorama. When he saw a man he wanted to shoot he brought him up to the cross-lines, and then pressed a finger upon a little push like an electric bell-push, conveniently placed in the centre of the knob. Then the man was shot. If by any chance the rifleman missed his target he moved the knob a trifle, or readjusted his dividers, pressed the push, and got him the second time.

This rifle and its sights protruded from a porthole, exactly like a great number of other portholes that ran in a triple row under the eaves of the cover of the land ironclad. Each porthole displayed a rifle and sight in dummy, so that the real ones could only be hit by a chance shot, and if one was, then the young man below said 'Pshaw!' turned on an electric light, lowered the injured instrument into his camera, replaced the injured part, or put up a new rifle if the injury was considerable.

You must conceive these cabins as hung clear above the swing of the axles, and inside the big wheels upon which the great elephant-like feet were hung, and behind these cabins along the centre of the monster ran a central gallery into which they opened, and along which worked the big compact engines. It was like a long passage into which this throbbing machinery had been packed, and the captain stood about the middle, close to the ladder that led to his conning-tower, and directed the silent, alert engineers – for the most part by signs. The throb and noise of the engines mingled with the reports of the rifles and the intermittent clangour of the bullet hail upon the armour. Ever and again he would touch the wheel that raised his conning-tower, step up his ladder until his engineers could see nothing of him above the waist, and then come down again with orders. Two small electric lights were all the illumination of this space – they were placed to make him most clearly visible to his subordinates; the air was thick with the smell of oil and petrol, and had the war correspondent been suddenly transferred from the spacious dawn outside to the bowels of the apparatus he would have thought himself fallen into another world.

The captain, of course, saw both sides of the battle. When he raised his head into his conning-tower there were the dewy sunrise, the amazed and disordered trenches, the flying and falling soldiers, the depressed-looking groups of prisoners, the beaten guns; when he bent down again to signal 'half speed', 'quarter speed', 'half circle round towards the right', or what not, he was in the oil-smelling twilight of the ill-lit engine room. Close beside him on either side was the mouthpiece of a speaking-tube, and ever and again he would direct one side or other of his strange craft to 'Concentrate fire forward on gunners', or to 'clear out trench about a hundred yards on our right front.'

He was a young man, healthy enough but by no means sun-tanned, and of a type of feature and expression that prevails in His Majesty's Navy: alert, intelligent, quiet. He and his engineers and his riflemen all went about their work, calm and reasonable men. They had none of that flapping strenuousness of the half-wit in a hurry, that excessive strain upon the blood-vessels, that hysteria of effort which is so frequently regarded as the proper state of mind for heroic deeds.

For the enemy these young engineers were defeating they felt a certain qualified pity and a quite unqualified contempt. They regarded these big, healthy men they were shooting down precisely as these same big, healthy men might regard some inferior kind of native. They despised them for making war; despised their bawling patriotisms and their emotionality profoundly; despised them, above all, for the petty cunning and the almost brutish want of imagination their method of fighting displayed. 'If they *must* make war,' these young men thought, 'why in thunder don't they do it like sensible men?' They resented the assumption that their own side was too stupid to do anything more than play their enemy's game, that they were going to play this costly folly according to the rules of unimaginative men. They resented being forced to the trouble of making man-killing machinery; resented the alternative of having to massacre these people or endure their truculent yappings; resented the whole unfathomable imbecility of war.

Meanwhile, with something of the mechanical precision of a good clerk posting a ledger, the riflemen moved their knobs and pressed their buttons. ...

The captain of Land Ironclad Number Three had halted on the crest close to his captured half-battery. His lined-up prisoners stood hard by and waited for the cyclists behind to come for them. He surveyed the victorious morning through his conning-tower.

He read the general's signals. 'Five and Four are to keep among the guns to the left and prevent any attempt to recover them. Seven and Eleven and Twelve, stick to the guns you have got; Seven, get into position to command the guns taken by Three. Then, we're to do something else, are we? Six and One, quicken up to about ten miles an hour and walk round behind that camp to the levels near the river – we shall bag the whole crowd of them,' interjected the young man. 'Ah, here we are! Two and Three, Eight and Nine, Thirteen and Fourteen, space out to a thousand yards, wait for the word, and then go slowly to cover the advance of the cyclist infantry against any charge of mounted troops. That's all right. But where's Ten? Halloa! Ten to repair and get movable as soon as possible. They've broken up Ten!'

The discipline of the new war machines was business-like rather than pedantic, and the head of the captain came down out of the conning-tower to tell his men. 'I say, you chaps there. They've broken up Ten. Not badly, I think; but anyhow, he's stuck.'

But that still left thirteen of the monsters in action to finish up the broken army.

The war correspondent stealing down his gully looked back and saw them all lying along the crest and talking fluttering congratulatory flags to one another. Their iron sides were shining golden in the light of the rising sun.

## V

The private adventures of the war correspondent terminated in surrender about one o'clock in the afternoon, and by that time he had stolen a horse, pitched off it, and narrowly escaped being rolled upon; found the brute had broken its leg, and shot it with his revolver. He had spent some hours in the company of a squad of dispirited riflemen, had quarrelled with them about topography at last, and gone off by himself in a direction that should have brought him to the banks of the river and didn't. Moreover, he had eaten all his chocolate and found nothing in the whole world to drink. Also, it had become extremely hot. From behind a broken, but attractive, stone wall he had seen far away in the distance the defender-horsemen trying to charge cyclists in open order, with land ironclads outflanking them on either side. He had discovered that cyclists could retreat over open turf before horsemen with a sufficient margin of speed to allow of frequent dismounts and much terribly effective sharpshooting; and he had a sufficient persuasion that those horsemen, having charged their hearts out, had halted just beyond his range of vision and surrendered. He had been urged to sudden activity by a forward movement of one of those machines that had threatened to enfilade his wall. He had discovered a fearful blister on his heel.

He was now in a scrubby gravelly place, sitting down and meditating on his pocket-handkerchief, which had in some extraordinary way become in the last twenty-four hours extremely ambiguous in hue. 'It's the whitest thing I've got,' he said.

He had known all along that the enemy was east, west, and south of him, but when he heard war ironclads Numbers One and Six talking in their measured, deadly way not half a mile to the north he decided to make his own little unconditional peace without any further risks. He was for hoisting his white flag to a bush and taking up a position of modest obscurity near it, until someone came along. He became aware of voices, clatter, and the distinctive noises of a body of horse, quite near, and he put his handkerchief in his pocket again and went to see what was going forward.

The sound of firing ceased, and then as he drew near he heard the deep sounds of many simple, coarse, but hearty and noble-hearted soldiers of the old school swearing with vigour.

He emerged from his scrub upon a big level plain, and far away a fringe of trees marked the banks of the river. In the centre of the picture was a still intact road bridge, and a big railway bridge a little to the right. Two land ironclads rested, with a general air of being long, harmless sheds, in a pose of anticipatory peacefulness right and left of the picture, completely commanding two miles and more of the river levels. Emerged and halted a few yards from the scrub was the remainder of the defender's cavalry, dusty, a little disordered and obviously annoyed, but still a very fine show of men. In the middle distance three or four men and horses were receiving medical attendance, and nearer a knot of officers regarded the distant novelties in mechanism with profound distaste. Everyone was very distinctly aware of the twelve other ironclads, and of the multitude of townsmen soldiers, on bicycles or afoot, encumbered now by prisoners and captured war-gear but otherwise thoroughly effective, who were sweeping like a great net in their rear.

'Checkmate,' said the war correspondent, walking out into the open. 'But I surrender in the best of company. Twenty-four hours ago I thought war was impossible – and these beggars have captured the whole blessed army! Well! Well!' He thought of his talk with the young lieutenant. 'If there's no end to the surprises of science, the civilised people have it, of course. As long as their science keeps going they will necessarily be ahead of open-country men. Still. ...' He wondered for a space what might have happened to the young lieutenant.

The war correspondent was one of those inconsistent people who always want the beaten side to win. When he saw all these burly, sun-tanned horsemen, disarmed and dismounted and lined up; when he saw their horses unskilfully led away by the singularly not equestrian cyclists to whom they had surrendered; when he saw these truncated Paladins watching this scandalous sight, he forgot altogether that he had called these men 'cunning louts' and wished them beaten not four-and-twenty hours ago. A month ago he had seen that regiment in its pride going forth to war, and had been told of its terrible prowess, how it could charge in open order with each man firing from his saddle, and sweep before it anything else that ever came out to battle in any sort of order, foot or horse. And it had had to fight a few score of young men in atrociously unfair machines!

'Manhood *versus* Machinery' occurred to him as a suitable headline. Journalism curdles all one's mind to phrases.

He strolled as near the lined-up prisoners as the sentinels seemed disposed to permit and surveyed them and compared their sturdy proportions with those of their lightly built captors.

'Smart degenerates,' he muttered. 'Anæmic cockneydom.'

The surrendered officers came quite close to him presently, and he could hear the colonel's high-pitched tenor. The poor gentleman had spent three years of arduous toil upon the best material in the world perfecting that shooting from the saddle charge, and he was mourning with phrases of blasphemy, natural under the circumstances what one could be expected to do against this suitably consigned ironmongery.

'Guns,' said someone.

'Big guns they can walk round. You can't shift big guns to keep pace with them and little guns in the open they rush. I saw 'em rushed. You might do a surprise now and then – assassinate the brutes, perhaps –'

'You might make things like 'em.'

'What? *More* ironmongery? Us? …'

'I'll call my article,' meditated the war correspondent, "Mankind *versus* Ironmongery", and quote the old boy at the beginning.'

And he was much too good a journalist to spoil his contrast by remarking that the half-dozen comparatively slender young men in blue pyjamas who were standing about their victorious land ironclad, drinking coffee and eating biscuits, had also in their eyes and carriage something not altogether degraded below the level of a man.

# INTRODUCTION
'No Man's Land', Susan Gates
'Christmas Truce', Robert Graves

One Christmas day during the First World War, German and British troops declared a truce, climbed out of their trenches and played a game of football. In context of the millions who were killed during this war, a moment of such ordinariness was completely *extra*ordinary.

In each of these two stories a boy learns about the football match long after the war has ended, but the authors tell their tales very differently. In Robert Graves' story an old man recounts the tale. In Susan Gates' story the boy is thrust right into the action. It might be interesting to consider which story makes it easier to imagine being there, and which does a better job of teaching us something about war.

# NO MAN'S LAND

## Susan Gates

Jake ripped open his last present. He'd been hoping against hope, even though it wasn't ball-shaped. When he saw it was a pair of gloves, his face scrunched into a scowl.

'Where's my football?' he said.

'What?'

Mum poked her head out of the steamy kitchen. It was only just after breakfast but she was already cooking Christmas dinner. She'd got up at six o' clock that morning to put the turkey in.

'My football,' demanded Jake. 'You said I'd definitely get one for Christmas.'

'Did I?' said Mum vaguely, fanning herself to get some cool air. 'It's like a sauna in this kitchen.'

'I said I wanted one. And you promised.'

'Did I?' repeated Mum, looking as if she had more important things on her mind.

'I told and told you,' said Jake. He felt bad temper

blooming inside him, like an evil flower. And he'd been in a great mood when he got up this morning! 'I told you loads of times.'

'I can't remember that,' said Mum. She frowned suddenly. 'I've still got those potatoes to peel.'

'What was I supposed to do? Tattoo it up here?' Jake dragged a finger across his forehead. 'Like, "BUY JAKE A FOOTBALL"? I thought you were listening.'

He made an ugly face at the gloves. They were woolly, from his great-gran. She probably knitted them herself. He wouldn't have minded a cool pair from a skateboarding shop.

'Stupid gloves.' He chucked them across the room.

He knew he was taking a big risk. Mum wasn't the patient type at the best of times. But on Christmas mornings she could go off like a firework. That's what she did now.

'Don't you start!' she exploded. 'You ungrateful brat! You've got loads of nice presents. And you're moaning about not having a football. You should be ashamed of yourself! Some poor kid in a refugee camp would give his right arm for those gloves!'

Jake opened his mouth to protest. He wanted to explain. How he'd already told his mates he was getting a football. How it was all arranged. In twenty minutes, they were meeting him at the field for a game. What were they going to say when he turned up without a ball?

'But Mum!' he said.

She gave him that killer shark glare. The one that could shrivel you up. It meant, 'You think I'm giving you a hard time now? You haven't seen nothing yet. Any second now I'm going to blow like a volcano. Then you'd better run for cover.'

Jake backed down. Better not upset her. Mum had the whole family coming for Christmas dinner. She'd probably already started on the sherry. Dad was keeping out of the way, down the shed.

Reluctantly, Jake clamped his mouth shut. Mum hung around in the doorway, still looking dangerous. But then a timer went off in the kitchen, PING!

'My sprouts!' shouted Mum, and she ducked back into the steam.

'Phew, those sprouts saved my life,' said Jake, wiping imaginary sweat off his forehead.

It was no good. He was never going to get Mum to understand his bitter disappointment.

He stomped out the house, his shoulders hunched, and headed for the park.

'It's not fair!' he hissed through gritted teeth. He'd dropped loads of hints about that football. He'd even shown her the one he wanted in a shop window.

He gave a big sigh. 'And I thought she was taking it all in,' he said. There was a Coke can on the pavement. He gave it a vicious kick.

Mum had no idea what it was like. Every time he wanted a kick about, he had to wait for someone to turn up who had their own ball. That meant Bradley, who had about two brain cells. He always got the time wrong. He arrived after you'd got fed up and gone home. Or he went to the wrong place and waited for hours, wondering, *Why am I the only one here?* Or Harry, who was dead keen and always turned up right on time. But was absolute rubbish at football.

It was frosty. Ice sparkled on the pavement. Jake cupped his cold hands and puffed hot breath into them. He should have worn those Christmas gloves after all.

'Maybe they won't turn up,' he thought, hopefully.

Fat chance. Two were waiting already. Stamping about to keep themselves warm. They had new football strips on.

*They got what they wanted for Christmas,* thought Jake.

Three others were straggling across the park. Lenny was using his mobile.

*He's probably phoning my house,* thought Jake, *to say, 'We can't start without you. You're bringing the ball. Get your lazy butt out of bed.'*

But that reminded him. He'd asked for a mobile for Christmas too. One of the latest models. But he knew he'd never get that, not in a million years.

At the last minute, he veered away from the field, dodged through some bushes. He just couldn't face his mates. It was too embarrassing.

'They'll think I was lying again,' he told himself. Sometimes he did lie, saying he'd got things his Mum and Dad couldn't afford. He'd got into big trouble with that trail bike. 'Yeah, my dad bought me it,' he'd boasted. And, of course, they'd all begged, 'Give us a ride on it!' He'd had to do even more lying, to get out of that one.

He felt sorry for himself. 'All I wanted this time was one crappy football!' It wasn't like he was asking for the world.

He didn't want to go home yet. So he knocked on Great-Gran's door. She lived in the old people's bungalows, just outside the park. She looked surprised when he walked in. She was still in her dressing gown.

'It's not that time already, is it?' she said. 'I thought your dad was picking me up at twelve.'

'He is,' said Jake, slumping into a chair. 'I'm here on my own. Got any microchips?'

After he'd glugged red sauce on his chips and slotted a few into his mouth, he felt happier.

'Hey, thanks for the gloves,' he told Great-Gran, grudgingly.

'Did you get some nice presents? Things you wanted?'

'I didn't get a football.' He just couldn't help blurting it out. 'And Mum practically promised me one.'

'That's a shame,' said Great-Gran, grieving along with him. Then her look brightened. 'Wait a minute,' she said. 'I've got a football somewhere.'

Jake stared at her, a microchip halfway to his mouth. 'Have you?'

*Magic*, was his first thought. Then he thought again. 'What kind of football?' he asked her, suspiciously. Great-Gran knew nothing about footballs. It was probably a little kids' blow-up beach ball. It was probably one she'd knitted.

'Oh, it's a proper one,' said Great-Gran, as if she was reading his mind. She bustled out of the room. He heard her rummaging around in the cupboard under the stairs. 'It belonged to your great-great-grandad.'

'Who?' said Jake.

'My dad,' explained Great-Gran, coming back with a dusty cardboard box. 'I haven't looked at it for donkey's years.'

She lifted it out of the box.

'It just needs pumping up a bit,' she said.

Jake groaned. Why had he got his hopes up? It was a proper football all right. It was even made of leather. But it was a joke. It was the saddest, scabbiest, most scuffed football Jake had ever seen. He couldn't help grinning.

'Gran! It's a mess. It looks like a dog's been chewing it. I can't take that down the park. My mates would fall about laughing.'

Great-Gran looked hurt. 'Is it no good then? I suppose it is a bit old.'

'How old?' asked Jake.

Great-Gran did some counting up in her head. 'About ninety years old.'

Jake burst out laughing. 'Gran! It's as old as you. It's ancient. It ought to be on the Antiques Roadshow.'

Great-Gran looked hurt again.

Just to please her, Jake pretended to be interested in the football. He took it from her.

'Ow!'

As soon as he touched it, a cold tingling feeling surged up his arms. When it reached the back of his neck, it made the hairs lift, like they do when you're scared. But what was there to be scared of? He was safe, here, in Great-Gran's bungalow. She even had an alarm, to call the warden.

Quickly, he put the ball down. He rubbed his tingling arms. He picked up his box of chips. But he couldn't shake off that strange feeling of dread. He even looked over his shoulder, as if there were someone hiding behind his chair.

'Put that ball away, Gran,' he shuddered. 'I don't want it. Put it back in the box.'

But Great-Gran had gone all misty-eyed. She was caught up in memories. She'd got something else out the box. It was a tatty yellow piece of paper.

'This was the letter his mate brought back, when he came home on leave from the Great War.'

'What war is that?' said Jake. His history was a bit hazy.

'It's the First World War I'm talking about,' said Great-Gran. 'Nineteen-fourteen to nineteen-eighteen. My dad was a soldier in that war. He fought the Germans. Except for Christmas Day, 1914. When he played football with them.'

'Played football with the German soldiers?' said Jake, confused. 'Weren't they supposed to be killing each other?'

'Not on Christmas Day,' said Gran. 'There was a truce.'

She unfolded the letter. It seemed as fragile as a cobweb. She put on her reading glasses. Jake fidgeted. He'd suddenly got itchy feet. 'Got to go now, Gran,' he said.

Great-Gran took no notice. She pursed her lips, following the lines on the letter with her finger.

'There's some bits Dad wrote about the rats and the mud and the fighting and how awful it was in the trenches. But here's the part about that football game.'

Gran read it, in a high warbly voice, sometimes stumbling over the words.

'The dawn was freezing cold and foggy at first. It was dead quiet, without the shells and the guns. My mates said, "You're barmy." I don't know what made me do it. But I just stood up on the parapet and no one shot me! So I took my football and went out into No Man's Land. I saw Fritz poking his head above his parapet so I gives the ball a kick and says, "Fancy a game, Fritz?" and blow me someone says, "OK, Tommy." And they all comes trooping out, real friendly. We even shake hands, like we hadn't been blasting each other to kingdom come the day before!'

Great-Gran stopped reading. She folded the letter up again.

Jake jumped to his feet. 'Can I borrow that ball, Gran?' He'd forgotten how even touching it had spooked him, seconds ago.

Great-Gran looked surprised, 'I thought you didn't want it.'

'Yeah, but that was before. Before I knew my great-great-grandad was a soldier. And that he had a kick about with some Germans on Christmas Day. I want to show my mates. This football is famous!'

He scooped up the ball. Again that chilly shiver ran up his arms. As if some kind of connection were being made. But he hardly noticed. He was more excited now than scared.

'Can I have the letter too?' He reached out to take it but Great-Gran drew it back.

'I think I'll keep it here,' she said.

For a second Jake was indignant. Great-Gran never said no. She always let him have anything he wanted. 'Why?' he frowned.

'Because I don't want nothing to happen to it. I told you, Dad's best mate brought it back for his family, along with this football and some of his other things. My dad never got the chance to post this letter,' said Great-Gran, her face suddenly filling with sadness. 'He got shot. Boxing Day, 1914, when I was just a baby.'

'Wow!' said Jake, excited. 'So that letter got found on his body? Are those bloodstains?' This was going to make a great story to tell his mates. They might even forget that he hadn't got a new football.

'Catch you later, Gran.'

Leaving Great-Gran still lost in her memories, he went speeding up the path. He was pleased to be outside. It was too hot and stuffy in Great-Gran's house. After about twenty minutes talking to her, he always wanted to escape.

He raced back to the park, with the football under

his arm. Were his mates still there? Some had gone home. But three or four were still hanging around, their breath making white clouds in the frosty air.

'Hey, you guys, guess what I've got?' he shouted.

The faces they turned towards him weren't welcoming.

'So you decided to turn up,' said Lenny, sarcastically. 'We've been freezing to death, waiting for you. You said ten o clock.'

Jake held out the football, 'I've got this, though.'

There was dead silence. Then someone hooted with laughter. And Lenny said, in disgust, 'You trying to be funny or what? You keep us waiting for ages. Then you turn up with that?'

'No, no,' said Jake, struggling to explain. 'You don't understand. It's not to play with. It's an antique. I just bought it to show you. It's a famous football. My great-great-grandad, he was a soldier. Right? And he played a game with the Germans, with this football, in the First World War.'

'So?' said Lenny, still in the same sarcastic voice.

And someone else said, 'Does that mean you didn't get a new football? Just like you didn't get that trail bike? So you're making up some kind of stupid lie. About a famous football or something?'

'Yeah,' added Lenny. 'Look at the state of it. He probably picked it out of a skip on the way here.'

'I didn't. I didn't,' spluttered Jake, his face turning bright red. 'And I'm not lying.'

But they were already walking away. They didn't once look back. They disappeared through the big, iron gates. There was no one else around, not even dog-walkers. He was alone, in an empty park, on a frozen football field.

Suddenly, the football felt as heavy as a boulder in his arms. Jake dropped it on to the grass. Why had he brought it to show them? He must have had a brainstorm. He should have known they'd just make fun of it.

'Stupid football.' He gave it a kick.

There was no chance of a game now. He had no one to play with. He shivered and hugged himself. It was getting colder. The kind of cold that went right through to your bones.

'Might as well go home,' he muttered to himself.

Fed up, he gave the football another boot.

There was a strange mist creeping towards him across the grass. Where had that come from? It curled and writhed like snakes. It lapped around his shoes in creamy waves.

Suddenly, he realized, he'd lost the football. The mist had swallowed it. That football was a family heirloom. Great-Gran would go mad!

But the mist was rising, getting thicker. First the

trees were fuzzy black shapes. Then they vanished altogether. Now, there were white cotton-wool walls closing in on him. Jake blundered about in the fog, his sense of direction totally scrambled.

'Aaargh!'

He was teetering on the edge of a big crater. His arms whirled like windmills. He saved himself, just in time, from slithering down the sides. What was that doing there? There should be barriers to keep kids from falling in. There should be signs saying, 'DANGER. KEEP OUT.'

The bottom was full of slushy mud. It looked like lumpy, yellow porridge.

'You could drown in there!' Jake gasped, horrified.

And, if anyone heard your cries for help, in this fog they wouldn't be able to find you. When he stretched out his arm, he couldn't even see his own fingers, waggling in front of his face.

He stumbled into a muddy rut. It had frozen, hard as iron. What had happened to their football field? It hadn't been smooth before. But now it was like a construction site.

*Where am I?* thought Jake. He didn't know this part of the park. He felt scared, totally disorientated.

'You've got to get out of here,' he told himself. 'Find the park gates.' Even a bench, or a litter bin would be something familiar.

Then something rolled slowly towards his foot. His toe stopped it. He looked down. It was the football, lying in an icy puddle. Someone had just kicked it back to him.

Those hairs on the back of his neck weren't just lifting now. They were wriggling about, like maggots.

'Who's there?' he shouted, trying to peer through the smoky swirls. Maybe one of his mates had come back, looking for him.

'Who's there?' he shouted again. 'Is that you, Lenny?'

His eyes screwed up. What was that? He could see twinkling lights in the fog. A row of twinkling lights, floating high up above the ground.

'What's happening?' Jake thought, panic-stricken. 'What is this place?'

Then a voice drifted through the freezing, foggy air.

'Merry Christmas, Tommy!'

*My name's not Tommy,* thought Jake, bewildered.

He stumbled into something. It was a bunch of tunic jackets, some khaki, some grey, piled up in a heap. There was another heap over there. He could just make it out, through the haze.

He and his mates often piled up their hoodies and jackets like that.

*It looks like ... goalposts,* thought Jake, frowning.

'Pass that ruddy ball, Fritz!'

Without thinking, Jake reacted. He booted the ball. Instantly the fog around him was full of running figures. The ball came back to him.

Jake started running too. But he kept the ball at his feet. He booted it again. It curved off into the mist. The figures around were keeping up with him. He was in a football game! He couldn't see faces, only shapes. But they were laughing, shouting, skidding on ice.

'Over here!' shouted Jake wildly, all flushed and excited. And someone passed him the ball. With a mighty kick, he belted it back into the fog.

'Goal!' someone yelled. 'Well done, Tommy!'

*Hey,* thought Jake. *I'm doing good here.*

'Look out, Jake!'

Who'd shouted that? It was an English voice. It came out of the fog and stopped him pitching head-first into another huge crater. He flung himself down, just in time, at its icy edge. But he slid forward so he was almost overhanging it, staring into its depths.

'No!' There were things floating in the mud. He didn't want to look. An arm sticking out, a boot. The back of someone's head. There were dead soldiers down there!

Jake scrambled up. He thought, *I'm gonna be sick.* His legs felt as wonky as a newborn foal's.

Then, out of the fog, Great-Great-Grandad's football trickled gently towards him. It stopped at his feet.

Suddenly, he found the strength to run. He snatched up the ball and hared off. Soon, he was on smoother ground, dodging through the fog, slamming into trees and park benches. Until he was hanging, half-hysterical, on to the park gates, gasping for breath, his heart hammering.

'You all right, son?' said someone. It was an old guy, walking his dog.

Jake could hardly speak. He pointed a shaking finger. 'Out there! Out there! Look!'

Together, they stared into the park. The fog had gone. There were only a few wispy rags left.

'What you on about, son?' the man said.

'Can't you see?' screamed Jake. 'It's No Man's Land!'

But No Man's Land had gone too. The litter bins, benches, and trees were back. The park looked just the same as it always did. Except the sun had come out over their football field. Making the ice crystals on the grass sparkle like jewels.

His brain numb, Jake trudged back to Great-Gran's, carrying the football. He couldn't think, daren't think, about what had just happened. And what he'd seen.

The ball was soggy now, heavy to carry. It made his arms ache.

Jake plodded wearily into Great-Gran's living room.

'Take those shoes off!' said Great-Gran straightaway. 'You're making a right mess of my carpets!'

Dazed, Jake looked down. His trainers were caked with thick yellow mud. There was no mud that colour round here.

'Where've you been?' fussed Great-Gran. 'In a mud bath? Look at your clothes. Your mum's going to have a fit.'

Jake slumped into a chair.

'Here's your ball back,' he said to Great-Gran. He wiped some mud off it with his sleeve. Then put it gently on the coffee table.

'You know,' said Great-Gran, 'after you'd gone, I had a proper read of Dad's letter. Would you believe it, them Germans put up trees at Christmas? On top of their trenches, all among the barbed wire? They even lit candles on the branches. They looked real pretty, Dad said, twinkling through the morning mist.'

'I saw them,' said Jake, speaking as if he was in a trance. 'And we played football. And someone knew my name, Gran. Someone called out to warn me.'

'What, my pet?' said Great-Gran, looking totally baffled.

Jake sighed. He shook himself like a wet dog.

'Never mind, Gran,' he said. 'I'm just talking rubbish.'

Had he really played football with ghosts in No Man's Land? And had his own great-great-grandad called out to him? To save him from falling into a shell hole full of corpses?

He shivered. His brain couldn't cope with that. Best not to think about it. Block it right out of his mind. Pretend it never happened. But there was one thing to say before he did.

'Put that football back in the box, Gran,' he begged. 'And don't take it out again, ever.'

'I'll buy you a brand new one, pet,' offered Great-Gran, shutting the ball away and closing the box lid. 'You can come with me. Show me which one you want.'

'Thanks, Gran,' said Jake, pleased.

'But we won't be able to get it until the shops open, after Christmas.'

'That's OK,' Jake told her. 'It's not that important. I can wait.'

# CHRISTMAS TRUCE

## Robert Graves

Young Stan comes around yesterday about tea-time – you know my grandson Stan? He's a Polytechnic student, just turned twenty, as smart as his dad was at the same age. Stan's all out to be a commercial artist and do them big coloured posters for the hoardings. Doesn't answer to 'Stan', though – says it's 'common'; says he's either 'Stanley' or he's nothing.

Stan's got a bagful of big, noble ideas; all schemed out carefully, with what he calls 'captions' attached.

Well, I can't say nothing against big, noble ideas. I was a red-hot Labour-man myself for a time, forty years ago now, when the Kayser's war ended and the war-profiteers began treading us ex-heroes into the mud. But that's all over long ago – in fact, Labour's got a damn sight too respectable for my taste! Worse than Tories, most of their leaders is now – especially them that used to be the loudest in rendering 'We'll Keep the

Red Flag Flying Still'. They're all Churchwardens now, or country gents, if they're not in the House of Lords.

Anyhow, yesterday Stan came around, about a big Ban-the-Bomb march all the way across England to Trafalgar Square. And couldn't I persuade a few of my old comrades to form a special squad with a banner marked 'First World War Veterans Protest Against the Bomb'? He wanted us to head the parade, ribbons, crutches, wheelchairs and all.

I put my foot down pretty hard. 'No, Mr Stanley,' I said politely, 'I regret as I can't accept your kind invitation.'

'But why?' says he. 'You don't want another war, Grandfather, do you? You don't want mankind to be annihilated? This time it won't be just a few unlucky chaps killed, like Uncle Arthur in the First War, and Dad in the Second ... It will be all mankind.'

'Listen, young 'un,' I said. 'I don't trust nobody who talks about mankind – not parsons, not politicians, not anyone else. There ain't no such thing as "mankind", not practically speaking there ain't.'

'Practically speaking, Grandfather,' says young Stan, 'there *is*. Mankind means all the different nations lumped together – us, the Russians, the Americans, the Germans, the French, and all the rest of them. If the bomb goes off, everyone's finished.'

'It's not going off,' I says.

'But it's gone off twice already – at Hiroshima and Nagasaki,' he argues, 'so why not again? The damage will be definitely final when it *does* go off.'

I wouldn't let Stan have the last word. 'In the crazy, old-fashioned war in which I lost my foot,' I said, a bit sternly, 'the Fritzes used poison gas. They thought it would help 'em to break through at Wipers. But somehow the line held, and soon our factories were churning out the same stinking stuff for us to use on them. All right, and now what about Hitler's war?'

'What about it?' Stan asks.

'Well,' I says, 'everyone in England was issued an expensive mask in a smart-looking case against poison-gas bombs dropped from the air – me, your dad, your ma, and yourself as a tiny tot. But how many poison-gas bombs were dropped on London, or on Berlin? Not a damned one! Both sides were scared stiff. Poison-gas had got too deadly. No mask in the market could keep the new sorts out. So there's not going to be no atom bombs dropped neither, I tell you, Stanley my lad; not this side of the Hereafter! Everyone's scared stiff again.'

'Then why do both sides manufacture quantities of atom bombs and pile them up?' he asks.

'Search me,' I said, 'unless it's a clever way of keeping up full employment by making believe there's a war on. What with bombs and fall-out shelters, and radar equipment, and unsinkable aircraft-carriers, and satellites, and shooting rockets at the moon, and keeping up big armies – takes two thousand quid nowadays to maintain a soldier in the field, I read the other day – what with all that play-acting, there's full employment assured for everyone, and businessmen are rubbing their hands.'

'Your argument has a bad flaw, Grandfather. The Russians don't need to worry about full employment.'

'No,' said I, 'perhaps they don't. But their politicians and commissars have to keep up the notion of a wicked Capitalist plot to wipe out the poor workers. And they have to show that they're well ahead in the Arms Race. Forget it, lad, forget it! Mankind, which is a term used by maiden ladies and bun-punchers, ain't going to be annihilated by no atom bomb.'

Stan changed his tactics. 'Nevertheless, Grandfather,' he says, 'we British want to show the Russians that we're not engaged in any such Capitalist plot. All men are brothers, and I for one have nothing against my opposite number in Moscow, Ivan. Whoever-he-may-be ... This protest march is the only logical way I can show him my dislike of organized propaganda.'

'But Ivan Orfalitch ain't here to watch you march; nor the Russian telly ain't going to show him no picture of it. If Ivan thinks you're a bleeding Capitalist, then he'll go on thinking you're a bleeding Capitalist; and he won't be so far out, neither, in my opinion. No, Stan, you can't fight organized propaganda with amachoor propaganda.

'Oh, can it, Grandfather!' says Stan. 'You're a professional pessimist. And *you* didn't hate the Germans even when you were fighting them – in spite of the newspapers. What about that Christmas Truce?'

Well, I'd mentioned it to him one day, I own; but it seems he'd drawn the wrong conclusions and didn't want to be put straight. However, I'm a lucky bloke – always being saved by what other blokes call 'coincidences', but which I don't; because they always happen when I need 'em most. In the trenches we used to call that 'being in God's pocket'. So, of course, we hear a knock at the door and a shout, and in steps my old mucking-in chum Dodger Green, formerly 301691, Pte Edward Green of the 1st Batt., North Wessex Regiment – come to town by bus for a Saturday-night booze with me, every bit of twenty miles.

'You're here in the exact nick, Dodger,' says I, 'as once before.' He'd nappooed a Fritz officer one day when I was lying with one foot missing outside Delville Wood, and the Fritz was kindly putting us wounded out of our misery with an automatic pistol.

'What's new, Fiddler?' he asks.

'Tell this lad about the *two* Christmas truces,' I said. 'He's trying to enlist us for a march to Moscow, or somewhere.'

'Well,' says Dodger, 'I don't see no connexion, not yet. And marching to Moscow ain't no worse nor marching to Berlin, same as you and me did – and never got more nor a few hundred yards forward in the three years we were at it. But, all right, I'll give him the facts, since you particularly ask me.'

Stan listened quietly while Dodger told his tale. I'd heard it often enough before, but Dodger's yarns improve with the telling. You see, I missed most of that first Christmas Truce, as I'll explain later. But I came in for the second; and saw a part of it what Dodger didn't. And the moral I wanted to impress on young Stan depended on there being *two* truces, not one: them two were a lot different from one another.

I brings a quart bottle of wallop from the kitchen, along with a couple of glasses – not three, because young Stan don't drink anything so 'common' as beer – and Dodger held forth. Got a golden tongue, has Dodger – I've seen him hold an audience spellbound at The Three Feathers from opening-time to stoptap, and his glass filled every ten minutes, free.

'Well,' he says, 'the first truce was in 1914, about four months after the Kayser's war began. They say that the old Pope suggested it, and that the Kayser agreed, but that Joffre, the French C-in-C wouldn't allow it. However, the Bavarians were sweating on a short spell of peace and goodwill, being Catholics, and sent word around that the Pope was going to get his way. Consequently, though we didn't have the Bavarians in front of us, there at Boy Greneer, not a shot was fired on our sector all Christmas Eve. In those days we hadn't been issued with Mills bombs, or trench-mortars, or Very pistols, or steel helmets, or sandbags, or any of them later luxuries; and only two machine-guns to a battalion. The trenches were shallow and knee-deep in water, so that most of the time we had to crouch on the fire step. God knows how we kept alive and smiling ... It wasn't no picnic, was it, Fiddler? – and the ground half-frozen, too!

'Christmas Eve, at seven thirty p.m., the enemy trenches suddenly lit up with a row of coloured Chinese lanterns and a bonfire started in the village behind. We stood to arms, prepared for whatever happened. Ten minutes later the Fritzes began singing a Christmas carol called "Stilly Nucked". Our boys answered with "Good King Wenceslas", which they'd learned the first verse of as Waits, collecting coppers from door to door. Unfortunately no one knew more than two verses, because Waits always either get a curse or a copper before they reach the third verse.

'Then a Fritz with a megaphone shouts, "Merry Christmas, Wessex!"

'Captain Pomeroy was commanding us. Colonel Baggie had gone sick, second-in-command still on leave, and most of the other officers were young second-lieutenants straight from Sandhurst – we'd taken such a knock, end of October. The Captain was a real gentleman: father, grandfather and greatgrandfather all served in the Wessex. He shouts back: "Who are you?" And they say that they're Saxons, same as us, from a town called Hully in West Saxony.

'"Will your commanding officer meet me in no man's land to arrange a Christmas truce?" the Captain shouts again. "We'll respect a white flag," he says.

'That was arranged, so Captain Pomeroy and the Fritz officer, whose name was Lieutenant Coburg, climbed out from their trenches and met half-way. They didn't shake hands, but they saluted, and each gave the other word of honour that his troops wouldn't fire a shot for another twenty-four hours. Lieutenant Coburg explained that his Colonel and all the senior officers were back taking it easy at Regimental HQ. It seems they liked to keep their boots clean, and their hands warm: not like our officers.

'Captain Pomeroy came back pleased as Punch, and said: "The truce starts at dawn, Wessex; but meanwhile we stay in trenches. And if any man of you dares break the truce tomorrow," he says, "I'll shoot him myself, because I've given that German officer my word. All the same, watch out, and don't let go of your bundooks."

'That suited us; we'd be glad to get up from them damned fire steps and stretch our legs. So that night we serenaded the Fritzes with all manner of songs, such as "I want to go Home!" and "The Top of the Dixie Lid", and the one about "Old Von Kluck, He Had a Lot of Men"; and they serenaded us with "*Deutschland Über Alles*", and songs to the concertina.

'We scraped the mud off our puttees and shined our brasses, to look a bit more regimental next morning. Captain Pomeroy, meanwhile, goes out again with a flashlight and arranges a Christmas football match – kick-off at ten thirty – to be followed at two o'clock by a burial service for all the corpses what hadn't been taken in because of lying too close to the other side's trenches.

'"Over the top with the best of luck!" shouts the Captain at eight a.m., the same as if he was leading an attack. And over we went, a bit shy of course, and stood there waiting for the Fritzes. They advanced to meet us, shouting, and five minutes later, there we were …

'Christmas was a peculiar sort of day, if ever I spent one. Hobnobbing with the Hun, so to speak: swapping fags and rum and buttons and badges for brandy, cigars and souvenirs. Lieutenant Coburg and several of the Fritzes talked English, but none of our blokes could sling a word of their bat.

'No man's land had seemed ten miles across when we were crawling out on a night patrol; but now we found it no wider than the width of two football pitches. We provided the football, and set up stretchers as goalposts; and the Reverend Jolly, our Padre, acted as ref. They beat us three–two, but the Padre had showed a bit too much Christian charity – their outside-left shot the deciding goal, but he was miles offside and admitted it soon as the whistle went. And we spectators were spread nearly two deep along the touch-lines with loaded rifles slung on our shoulders.

'We had Christmas dinner in our own trenches, and a German bugler obliged with the mess call – same tune as ours. Captain Pomeroy was invited across, but didn't think it proper to accept. Then one of our sentries, a farmer's son, sees a hare loping down the line between us. He gives a view halloo, and everyone rushes to the parapet and clambers out and runs forward to cut it off. So do the Fritzes. There ain't no such thing as harriers in Germany; they always use shot-guns on hares. But they weren't allowed to shoot this one, not with the truce; so they turned harriers same as us.

'Young Totty Fahy and a Saxon corporal both made a grab for the hare as it doubled back in their direction. Totty catches it by the forelegs and the Corporal catches it by the hindlegs, and they fall on top of it simultaneous.

'Captain Pomeroy looked a bit worried for fear of a shindy about who caught that hare; but you'd have laughed your head off to see young Totty and the Fritz both politely trying to force the carcase on each other! So the Lieutenant and the Captain gets together, and the Captain says: "Let them toss a coin for it." But the Lieutenant says: "I regret that our men will not perhaps understand. With us, we draw straws." So they picked some withered stems of grass, and Totty drew the long one. He was in our section, and we cooked the hare with spuds that night in a big iron pot borrowed from Duck Farm; but Totty gave the Fritz a couple of bully-beef tins, and the skin. Best stoo I ever ate!

'We called 'em "Fritzes" at that time. Afterwards they were "Jerries", on account of their tin hats. Them helmets with spikes called *Pickelhaubes* was still the issue in 1914, but only for parade use. In the trenches caps were worn; like ours, but grey, and no stiffening in the top. Our blokes wanted *pickelhaubes* badly to take their fiancées when they went home on leave; but Lieutenant Coburg says, sorry, all *pickelhaubes* was in store behind the lines. They had to be content with belt-buckles.

'General French commanded the BEF at the time – decent old stick. Said afterwards that if he'd been consulted about the truce, he'd have agreed for chivalrous reasons. He must have reckoned that whichever side beat, us or the Germans, a Christmas truce would help considerably in signing a decent peace at the finish. But the Kayser's High Command were mostly Prussians, and Lieutenant Coburg told us that the Prussians were against the truce, which didn't agree with their "frightfulness" notions; and though other battalions were fraternizing with the Fritzes up and down the line that day – but we didn't know it – the Prussians weren't having any. Nor were some English regiments: such as the East Lanes on our right flank and the Sherwood Foresters on the left – when the Fritzes came out with white flags, they fired over their heads and waved 'em back. But they didn't interfere with our party. It was worse in the French line: them Frogs machine-gunned all the "Merry Christmas" parties … Of course, the French go in for New Year celebrations more than Christmas.

'One surprise was the two barrels of beer that the Fritzes rolled over to us from the brewery just behind their lines. I don't fancy French beer; but at least this wasn't watered like what they sold us English troops in the *estaminets*. We broached them out in the open, and the Fritzes broached another two of their own.

'When it came to the toasts, the Captain said he wanted to keep politics out of it. So he offered them "Wives and Sweethearts!" which the Lieutenant accepted. Then the Lieutenant proposed "The King!" which the Captain accepted. There was a King of Saxony too, you see, in them days, besides a King of England; and no names were mentioned. The third toast was "A Speedy Peace!" and each side could take it to mean victory for themselves.

'After dinner came the burial service – the Fritzes buried their corpses on their side of the line; we buried ours on ours. But we dug the pits so close together that one service did for both. The Saxons had no Padre with them; but they were Protestants, so the Reverend Jolly read the service, and a German divinity student translated for them. Captain Pomeroy sent for the drummers and put us through that parade in proper regimental fashion: slow march, arms reversed, muffled drums, a Union Jack and all.

'An hour before dark, a funny-faced Fritz called Putzi came up with a trestle table. He talked English like a Yank. Said he'd been in Ringling's Circus over in the United States. Called us "youse guys", and put on a hell of a good gaff with conjuring tricks and juggling

– had his face made up like a proper clown. Never heard such applause as we gave Herr Putzi!

'Then, of course, our bastard of a Brigadier, full of turkey and plum pudding and mince pies, decides to come and visit the trenches to wish us Merry Christmas! Captain Pomeroy got the warning from Fiddler here, who was away down on light duty at Battalion HQ. Fiddler arrived in the nick, running split-arse across the open, and gasping out: "Captain, sir, the Brigadier's here; but none of us hasn't let on about the truce."

'Captain Pomeroy recalled us at once. "*Imshi*, Wessex!" he shouted. Five minutes later the Brigadier came sloshing up the communication trench, keeping his head well down. The Captain tried to let Lieutenant Coburg know what was happening; but the Lieutenant had gone back to fetch him some warm gloves as a souvenir. The Captain couldn't speak German; what's more, the Fritzes were so busy watching Putzi that they wouldn't listen. So Captain Pomeroy shouts to me: "Private Green, run along the line and order the platoon commanders from me to fire three rounds rapid over the enemies' heads." Which I did; and by the time the Brigadier turns up, there wasn't a Fritz in sight.

'The Brigadier, whom we called "Old Horseflesh", shows a lot of Christmas jollity. "I was very glad," he says, "to hear that Wessex fusillade, Pomeroy. Rumours have come in of fraternization elsewhere along the line. Bad show! Disgraceful! Can't interrupt a war for freedom just because of Christmas! Have you anything to report?"

'Captain Pomeroy kept a straight face. He says: "Our sentries report that the enemy have put up a trestle table in no man's land, sir. A bit of a puzzle, sir. Seems to have a bowl of goldfish on it." He kicked the Padre, and the Padre kept his mouth shut.

'Old Horseflesh removes his brass hat, takes his binoculars, and cautiously peeps over the parapet. "They *are* goldfish, by Gad!" he shouts. "I wonder what new devilish trick the Hun will invent next. Send out a patrol tonight to investigate." "Very good, sir," says the Captain.

'Then Old Horseflesh spots something else: it's Lieutenant Coburg strolling across the open between his reserve and front lines; and he's carrying the warm gloves. "What impudence! Look at that swaggering German officer! Quick, here's your rifle, my lad! Shoot him down point-blank!" It seems Lieutenant Coburg must have thought that the fusillade came from the Foresters on our flank; but now he suddenly stopped short and looked at no man's land, and wondered where everyone was gone.

'Old Horseflesh shoves the rifle into my hand.

"Take a steady aim," he says. "Squeeze the trigger, don't pull!" I aimed well above the Lieutenant's head and fired three rounds rapid. He staggered and dived head-first into a handy shell-hole.

'"Congratulations," said Old Horseflesh, belching brandy in my face. "You can cut another notch in your rifle butt. But what effrontery! Thought himself safe on Christmas Day, I suppose! Ha, ha!" He hadn't brought Captain Pomeroy no gift of whisky or cigars, nor nothing else; stingy bastard, he was. At any rate, the Fritzes caught on, and their machine-guns began traversing tock-tock-tock, about three feet above our trenches. That sent the Brigadier hurrying home in such a hurry that he caught his foot in a loop of telephone wire and went face forward into the mud. It was his first and last visit to the front line.

'Half an hour later we put up an ALL CLEAR board. This time us and the Fritzes became a good deal chummier than before. But Lieutenant Coburg suggests it would be wise to keep quiet about the lark. The General Staff might get wind of it and kick up a row, he says. Captain Pomeroy agrees. Then the Lieutenant warns us that the Prussian Guards are due to relieve his Saxons the day after Boxing Day. "I suggest that we continue the truce until then, but with no more fraternization," he says. Captain Pomeroy agrees again. He accepts the warm gloves and in return gives the Lieutenant a

Shetland wool scarf. Then he asks whether, as a great favour, the Wessex might be permitted to capture the bowl of goldfish, for the Brigadier's sake. Herr Putzi wasn't too pleased, but Captain Pomeroy paid him for it with a gold sovereign and Putzi says: "Please, for Chrissake, don't forget to change their water!"

'God knows what the Intelligence made of them goldfish when they were sent back to Corps HQ, which was a French luxury *shadow* ... I expect someone decided the goldfish have some sort of use in trenches, like the canaries we take down the coal pits.

'Then Captain Pomeroy says to the Lieutenant: "From what I can see, Coburg, there'll be a stalemate on this front for a year or more. You can't crack our line, even with massed machine-guns; and we can't crack yours. Mark my words: our Wessex and your West Saxons will still be rotting here next Christmas – what's left of them."

'The Lieutenant didn't agree, but he didn't argue. He answered: "In that case, Pomeroy, I hope we both survive to meet again on that festive occasion; and that our troops show the same gentlemanly spirit as today."

'"I'll be very glad to do so," says the Captain, "if I'm not scuppered meanwhile." They shook hands on that, and the truce continued all Boxing Day. But nobody went out into no man's land, except at night to strengthen the wire where it had got trampled by the festivities. And of course we couldn't prevent our gunners from shooting; and neither could the Saxons prevent theirs. When the Prussian Guards moved in, the war started again; fifty casualties we had in three days, including young Totty who lost an arm.

'In the meantime a funny thing had happened: the sparrows got wind of the truce and came flying into our trenches for biscuit crumbs. I counted more than fifty in a flock on Boxing Day.

'The only people who objected strongly to the truce, apart from the Brigadier and a few more like him, was the French girls. Wouldn't have nothing more to do with us for a time when we got back to billets. Said we were *no bon* and *boko camarade* with the *Allemans*.'

Stan had been listening to this tale with eyes like stars. 'Exactly,' he said. 'There wasn't any feeling of hate between the individuals composing the opposite armies. The hate was all whipped up by the newspapers. Last year, you remember, I attended the Nürnberg Youth Rally. Two other fellows whose fathers had been killed in the last war, like mine, shared the same tent with four German war-orphans. They weren't at all bad fellows.'

'Well, lad,' I said, taking up the yarn where Dodger

left off, 'I didn't see much of that first Christmas Truce owing to a spent bullet what went into my shoulder and lodged under the skin: the Medico cut it out and kept me off duty until the wound healed. I couldn't wear a pack for a month, so, as Dodger told you, I got Light Duty down at Battalion HQ, and missed the fun. But the second Christmas Truce, now that was another matter. By then I was Platoon Sergeant to about twenty men signed on for the Duration of the War – some of them good, some of 'em His Majesty's bad bargains.

'We'd learned a lot about trench life that year; such as how to drain trenches and build dugouts. We had barbed wire entanglements in front of us, five yards thick, and periscopes, and listening-posts out at sap-heads; also trench-mortars and rifle-grenades, and bombs, and steel-plates with loop-holes for sniping through.

'Now I'll tell you what happened, and Dodger here will tell you the same. Battalion orders went round to Company HQ every night in trenches, and the CO was now Lieutenant-Colonel Pomeroy – DSO with bar. He'd won brevet rank for the job he did rallying the battalion when the big German mine blew C Company to bits and the Fritzes followed up with bombs and bayonets. However, when he sent round Orders two days before Christmas 1915, Colonel Pomeroy (accidentally on purpose) didn't tell the Adjutant to include the "Official Warning to All Troops" from General Sir Douglas Haig. Haig was our new Commander-in-Chief. You hear about him on Poppy Day – the poppies he sowed himself, most of 'em! He'd used his influence with King George, to get General French booted out and himself shoved into the job. His "Warning" was to the effect that any man attempting to fraternize with His Majesty's enemies on the poor excuse of Christmas would be court-martialled and shot. But Colonel Pomeroy never broke his word not even if he swung for it; and here he was alongside the La Bassée Canal, and opposite us were none other than the same West Saxons from Hully!

'The Colonel knew who they were because we'd coshed and caught a prisoner in a patrol scrap two nights before, and after the Medico plastered his head, the bloke was brought to Battalion HQ under escort (which was me and another man). The Colonel questioned him through an interpreter about the geography of the German trenches: where they kept that damned minny-werfer, how and when the ration parties came up, and so on. But this Fritz wouldn't give away a thing; said he'd lost his memory when he'd got coshed. So at last the Colonel remarked in English: "Very well that's all. By the way, is Lieutenant Coburg still alive?"

'"Oh, yeah," says the Fritz, surprised into talking English. "He's back again after a coupla wounds. He's a Major now, commanding our outfit."

'Then a sudden thought struck him. "For Chrissake," he says, "ain't you the Wessex officer who played Santa Claus last year and fixed that truce?"

'"I am," says the Colonel, "and you're Putzi Cohen the Conjurer, from whom I once bought a bowl of goldfish! It's a small war!"

'That's why, you see, the Colonel hadn't issued Haig's warning. About eighty or so of us old hands were still left, mostly snobs, bobbajers, drummers, transport men or wounded blokes rejoined. The news went the rounds, and they all rushed Putzi and shook his hand and asked couldn't he put on another conjuring gaff for them? He says: "Ask Colonel Santa Claus! He's still feeding my goldfish."

'I was Putzi's escort, before I happened to have coshed him and brought him in; but I never recognized him without his greasepaint – not until he started talking his funny Yank English.

'The Colonel sends for Putzi again, and says: "I don't think you're quite well enough to travel. I'm keeping you here as a hospital case until after Christmas."

'Putzi lived like a prize pig the next two days, and put on a show every evening – card tricks mostly, because he hadn't his accessories. Then came

Christmas Eve, and a sergeant of the Holy Boys who lay on our right flank again, remarked to me it was a pity that "Stern-Endeavour" Haig had washed out our Christmas fun. "First I've heard about it," says I, "and what's more, chum, I don't want to hear about it, see? Not officially, I don't."

'I'd hardly shut my mouth before them Saxons put out Chinese lanterns again and started singing "Stilly Nucked". They hadn't fired a shot, neither, all day.

'Soon word comes down the trench: "Colonel's orders: no firing as from now, without officer's permission."

'After stand-to next morning, soon as it was light, Colonel Pomeroy he climbed out of the trench with a white handkerchief in his hand, picked his way through our wire entanglements and stopped half-way across no man's land. "Merry Christmas, Saxons!" he shouted. But Major Coburg had already advanced towards him. They saluted each other and shook hands. The cheers that went up! "Keep in your trenches, Wessex!" the Colonel shouted over his shoulder. And the Major gave the same orders to his lot.

'After jabbering a bit they agreed that any bloke who'd attended the 1914 party would be allowed out of trenches, but not the rest – they could trust only us regular soldiers. Regulars, you see, know the rules of war and don't worry their heads about politics nor propaganda; them Duration blokes sickened us sometimes with their patriotism and their lofty skiting, and their hatred of "the Teuton foe" as one of 'em called the Fritzes.

'Twice more Saxons than Wessex came trooping out. We'd strict orders to discuss no military matters – not that any of our blokes had been studying German since the last party. Football was off, because of the overlapping shell holes and the barbed wire, but we got along again with signs and a bit of café French, and swapped fags and booze and buttons. But the Colonel wouldn't have us give away no badges. Can't say we were so chummy as before. Too many of ours and theirs had gone west that year and, besides, the trenches weren't flooded like the first time.

'We put on three boxing bouts: middle, welter and light; won the welter and light with KOs, lost the middle on points. Colonel Pomeroy took Putzi up on parole, and Putzi gave an even prettier show than before, because Major Coburg had sent back for his greasepaints and accessories. He used a parrakeet this time instead of goldfish.

'After dinner we found we hadn't much more to tell the Fritzes or swap with them, and the officers decided to pack up before we all got into trouble. The Holy Boys had promised not to shoot, and the left flank was screened by the Canal bank. As them two was busy discussing how long the no-shooting truce should last, all of a sudden the Christmas spirit flared up again. We and the Fritzes found ourselves grabbing hands and forming a ring around the pair of them – Wessex and West Saxons all mixed anyhow and dancing from right to left to the tune of "Here We Go Round the Mulberry Bush", in and out of shell holes. Then our RSM pointed to Major Coburg, and some of our blokes hoisted him on their shoulders and we all sang "For He's a Jolly Good Fellow". And the Fritzs hoisted our Colonel up on their shoulders too, and sang "*Hock Solla Leeben*", or something ... Our Provost-sergeant took a photo of that; pity he got his before it was developed.

'Now here's something I heard from Lightning Collins, an old soldier in my platoon. He'd come close enough to overhear the Colonel and the Major's conversation during the middle-weight fight when they thought nobody was listening. The Colonel says: "I prophesied last year, Major, that we'd still be here this Christmas, what was left of us. And now I tell you again that we'll still be here *next* Christmas, *and* the Christmas after. If we're not scuppered; and that's a ten to one chance. What's more, next Christmas there won't be any more fun and games and fraternization. I'm doubtful whether I'll get away with this present act of insubordination; but I'm a man of my word, as you are, and we've both kept our engagement."

"'Oh, yes, Colonel," says the Major. "I too will be lucky if I am not court-martialled. Our orders were as severe as yours." So they laughed like crows together.

'Putzi was the most envied man in France that day: going back under safe escort to a prison camp in Blighty. And the Colonel told the Major: "I congratulate you on that soldier. He wouldn't give away a thing!"

'At four o'clock sharp we broke it off; but the two officers waited a bit longer to see that everyone got back. But no, young Stan that's not the end of the story! I had a bloke in my platoon called Gipsy Smith, a dark-faced, dirty soldier, and a killer. He'd been watching the fun from the nearest sap-head, and no sooner had the Major turned his back than Gipsy aimed at his head and tumbled him over.

'The first I knew of it was a yell of rage from everyone all round me. I see Colonel Pomeroy run up to the Major, shouting for stretcher-bearers. Them Fritzes must have thought the job was premeditated, because when our stretcher-bearers popped out of the trench, they let 'em have it and hit one bloke in the leg. His pal popped back again.

'That left the Colonel alone in no man's land. He strolled calmly towards the German trenches, his hands in his pockets – being too proud to raise them over his head. A couple of Fritzes fired at him, but both missed. He stopped at their wire and shouted: "West Saxons, my men had strict orders not to fire. Some coward has disobeyed. Please help me carry the Major's body back to your trenches! Then you can shoot me, if you like; because I pledged my word that there'd be no fighting."

'The Fritzes understood, and sent stretcher-bearers out. They took the Major's body back through a crooked lane in their wire and Colonel Pomeroy followed them. A German officer bandaged the Colonel's eyes as soon as he got into the trench, and we waited without firing a shot to see what would happen next. That was about four o'clock, and nothing did happen until second watch. Then we see a flashlight signalling, and presently the Colonel comes back, quite his usual self.

'He tells us that, much to his relief, Gipsy's shot hadn't killed the Major but only furrowed his scalp and knocked him senseless. He'd come to after six hours, and when he saw the Colonel waiting there, he'd ordered his immediate release. They'd shaken hands again, and said: "Until after the war!", and the Major gives the Colonel his flashlight.

'Now the yarn's nearly over, Stan, but not quite. News of the truce got round, and General Haig ordered first an Inquiry and then a Court Martial on

Colonel Pomeroy. He wasn't shot, of course; but he got a severe reprimand and lost five years' seniority. Not that it mattered, because he got shot between the eyes in the 1916 Delville Wood show where I lost my foot.

'As for Gipsy Smith, he said he'd been obeying Haig's strict orders not to fraternize, and also he'd felt bound to avenge a brother killed at Loos. "Blood for blood," he said "is our gipsy motto." So we couldn't do nothing but show what we thought by treating him like the dirt he was. And he didn't last long. I sent Gipsy back with the ration party on Boxing Night. We were still keeping up our armed truce with the Saxons, but again their gunners weren't a party to it, and outside the Quartermaster's hut Gipsy got his backside removed by a piece of howitzer shell. Died on the hospital train, he did.

'Oh, I was forgetting to tell you that no sparrows came for biscuit crumbs that Christmas. The birds had all cleared off months before.

'Every year that war got worse and worse. Before it ended, nearly three years later, we'd have ten thousand officers and men pass through that one battalion, which was never at more than the strength of five hundred rifles. I'd had three wounds by 1916; some fellows got up to six before it finished. Only Dodger here came through without a scratch. That's how he got his name, dodging the bullet that had his name and number on it. The Armistice found us at Mons, where we started. There was talk of "Hanging the Kayser"; but they left him to chop wood in Holland instead. The rest of the Fritzes had their noses properly rubbed in the dirt by the Peace Treaty. But we let them rearm in time for a second war, Hitler's war, which is how your dad got killed. And after Hitler's war there'd have been a third war, just about now, which would have caught you, Stanley my lad, if it weren't for that blessed bomb you're asking me to march against.

'Now, listen, lad: if two real old-fashioned gentlemen like Colonel Pomeroy and Major Coburg – never heard of him again, but I doubt if he survived, having the guts he had – if two real men like them two couldn't hope for a third Christmas Truce in the days when "mankind", as you call 'em, was still a little bit civilized, tell me, what can you hope for now?

'Only fear can keep the peace,' I said. 'The United Nations are a laugh, and you know it. So thank your lucky stars that the Russians have H-bombs and that the Yanks have H-bombs, stacks of 'em, enough to blow your "mankind" up a thousand times over; and that everyone's equally respectful of everyone else, though not on regular visiting terms.'

I stopped, out of breath, and Dodger takes Stan by

the hand. 'You know what's right for *you*, lad?' he says, 'So don't listen to your granddad. Don't be talked out of your beliefs! He's one of the Old and Bold, but may be he's no wiser nor you and I.'

# INTRODUCTION
## 'Zakky', Robert Westall
## 'The Destructors', Graham Greene

Not all war stories show us the whites of enemy soldiers' eyes. War can affect people who are never on the front line. In Robert Westall's story, the narrator observes with growing concern the damage that war has wreaked on his Polish friend, Zakky. Although it is a bleak portrayal, the actions of the wider community provide some notes of hope.

'The Destructors' by Graham Greene has no explicit links to war. A group of teenagers execute a plan to destroy an old man's house – a house that survived the Blitz during the Second World War. The story was written less than 10 years after the end of the war and it is implicit that the teenagers and their behaviour are products of war. Looking to these boys' futures you could also read the story as a prediction of future war.

What do the violent acts in these two stories tell us about the impact of war, and what different predictions do they hold for the future?

# ZAKKY

## Robert Westall

Dad's Army?

I'll bet it made you laugh. But none of it was true, not round where I lived.

That rubbish about drilling with pitchforks and broom handles. Every lad in our village had his own shotgun by sixteen; been using one since he was ten. They could drop a half-grown rabbit at a hundred yards. What else d'you think they lived on? Farm-labourers' wages? All the government had to do was issue shot-gun cartridges containing one big solid shot, which would have blown a hole in Jerry big enough to put your hand through.

We had five gamekeepers in our lot; knew every spinney and gap in the hedge for miles. And twice as many poachers, fly enough to swipe the Lady Amherst pheasants off the terrace of Birleigh Manor, while his lordship sat there drinking afternoon tea. Brutal men, all of them. I've known some stagger home needing sixteen stitches in their head after some little encounter in the dark. They made peace while they were on Home Guard duty, and went back to their private war afterwards.

Yes, we did have a poet. Laurie Tomlinson. Professor somewhere now. But then he'd just got back from the Spanish Civil War. Showed us how to garrotte a man with a piece of piano wire so he died without a sigh. Showed the village blacksmith how to make a two-inch mortar from a yard of steel gas-piping. The army took those off us later, saying they were too dangerous to use. But they fired mortar-bombs all right; the ones Pincher Morton pinched from the Polish camp down the road.

And we never drilled in pinstripe suits or cricket shirts. We never wasted time drilling at all. We went on patrol in the washed-out browns and greys that poachers wore, which blend with the woodland at five paces. Laurie taught us how to put boot-polish on our faces so that it didn't crack and drop off like mud. Our village poachers still use boot-polish ...

And, poachers or not, they were all old *soldiers.* From the Last Lot. Hard-bodied farmhands of forty, who'd been snipers in the mud of the Somme, or bomb-throwers in the Ypres Salient. When we finally got our old Canadian rifles, dating from 1912, they nursed them like grim mothers. Very anxious to get their hands on the bayonets. First they sharpened them on their own whetstones, then they blackened them so no glint would give away their position.

All the young lads were mad to join. The veterans wouldn't have 'em. War wasn't for kids, they said. Forgetting they'd been little more than kids themselves in the Last Lot. We only ever had two young 'uns in our platoon. I was one.

I'd tried for a commission in our county regiment. Then for the RAF as anything. Even the navy, though I was seasick crossing to the Isle of Wight. But I had flat feet. When I put any weight on my feet, my toes pointed up in the air like ac-ac guns. Didn't count that I played rugger, and ran cross-country. I was *out*.

Went to see Major Newsam; asked if he'd pull a few strings for me with his old mates. He shook his head and told me the best thing I could do was to farm the land my father had left me as well as I damned well could. Damned U-boats would try to starve the country out, just like the Last Lot.

As a sop, he let me join his Home Guard. As second-in-command, with a pip on my shoulder.

'Old soldiers need someone to look up to,' he said. 'Someone to look after. Leave all the organizing to your platoon-sergeant. Never ask a man to do what you can't do yourself.'

It was a rule he kept himself, even though he'd lost half an arm in Iraq in 1924.

When they asked for Draggett's Mill as their HQ, I couldn't refuse. Right in the middle of my land; on the highest hill for miles, to make the best of the wind. But Draggett had been gone a long time, and the mill was just an empty stone shell, like a squat, blackened milk-bottle. They fitted it out with new floors and ladders, and with a parapet of sandbags and a corrugated iron roof, it made an ideal look-out for German paratroopers dropping in.

It was there, as we stood-to one lovely soft summer evening in 1940, that they dragged Zakky in. They'd caught him following them, and they thought he was a German spy. He'd put up a hell of a fight; three of them were bleeding. They'd had to knock him senseless with a rifle-butt. They poured water over him from our brew-up milk-churn, and he opened one swollen eye a green slit and said,

'*English!* If you had been Germans, I would have killed you all.'

'Nasty little sod, sir,' said Curly Millbank. 'He had this hidden under his shirt, at the back of his neck.' He passed me a simple flat knife, honed to a needle point.

'Give me my knife!' The thin wet figure on the floor

came at me so fast he knocked me clean across the trestle table that served as our office. All knees and elbows he was, and they felt as sharp as needles too. It took four of them to drag him off me, and somebody else got bitten.

'Who are you?' I asked, when I'd got my breath back.

'I am *soldier*.' He drew himself up to his full five foot three. 'Zbigniew Zakrewski, Polish Army.' He gabbled some long number. 'They give me a number. They had no rifles.'

'I think I've seen him hanging round the Polish camp, sir,' said Pincher Morton. 'The soldiers feed him. But he's not one of them.'

Zakky pulled a horrible face. 'I go to them. Tell them how to kill Nazis. They make me peel spuds.' He spat on our highly polished floor. 'That is why I follow your men. I will show *you* how to kill Nazis.'

He drew his hand across his throat.

Major Newsam came in then, and took over. I was still feeling a bit shaken.

'Checked up on him with the Poles,' Newsam told me at stand-to next evening. 'He's Polish all right. Thirteen years old. Joined the Polish Army in their retreat last September. Never had a rifle, never had a uniform. Marched five days, then met the Russkis coming the other way. Got away when the rest surrendered. Seems to have sneaked out through the Balkans and stowed away on a ship from Piraeus. Lot of Poles came that way. The Polish Government in exile tried putting him in a children's home, but he just kept running away. Apparently he eats at the Polish camp and sleeps in the woods. Keeps trying to nick weapons from their armoury. They're terrified he'll end up doing somebody an injury. I mean, all the Poles are fighting-mad, but he's got even them scared *silly*. They asked if I could get somebody to adopt him ...' He looked at me queryingly. 'Think your mother could take him on?'

Old Newsam was a bit sweet on my mother; thought she was wonder-woman.

I looked him straight in the eye. 'You'll have to bribe him. Let him join the Home Guard ...'

He grinned and said, 'Pity about your flat feet, Keith. You wouldn't have made a bad officer, given time.'

So I drove him home in my old farm van, the scruffy little tick. He ponged out the van to high heaven. When we got home, I heard my mother playing the piano. Chopin. She used to work like hell all day: the farm, evacuees, WVS, the lot. But when she was finally done for the day, she still liked to get dressed up a bit, and have a drink, and light the tall thin brass candles that stood on the piano, and play Chopin. Said it convinced her there'd be a better world again, some day.

I was going to march straight in and interrupt her, because I wanted to get back to the mill in case anything had happened while I'd been gone. But, in the half-open doorway, a small, steely hand caught my wrist. And Zakky just stood there till she had finished, the tears running down his cheek in the candle-light. It was the Chopin, I suppose.

When she had finished, and turned and smiled at us, he went straight up to her, clicked his heels together, and gave a funny little bow of his head. He was such an odd little scruff, I wondered how even a woman as wise as my mother would take it. But she took it all in her stride, shook him by the hand, and asked him if he'd care for a bath?

So I left her to get on with it. The next morning he came down to breakfast in one of my old grey school suits, white shirt and tie, long dark hair slicked down with tap water. Apparently she'd laid out the suit and shirt next to his pathetic rags on his bed, while he had a bath, and he'd chosen freely to wear them. Only he'd asked her to wash the rags for him, because they were Polish and precious. (And she spent hours mending them, as well.) And he'd showed her a solid gold locket, with a photo of a fierce, moustached military man on one side, and a rather lovely dark-haired woman on the other.

'My father. My mother.' He had clicked his heels again.

'Where are they now, Zakky?'

'Dead,' he said and took the locket back, and he never showed it to anybody else, ever. She said it was the only thing he had, except for the throwing knife that he still wore at the back of his neck, under the grey English suit.

I studied him over the bacon and eggs. I think his family must have been pretty well off, back in Poland, because he had exquisite table manners, only a little strange and foreign. And though he had the body of a half-starved kid, his face was ... ageless. Beaky nose, strong Polish cheekbones and a strong Polish jawbone, the sort you never see in an Englishman. His eyes were deep-sunken. They were either blazing with excitement, or too sad to look at direct.

They only blazed when he talked about Poland; or killing Nazis. Or when he was talking direct to my mother. In his eyes, my mother could do no wrong. He always called her Madam Bosworth, whether she was there or not. I think he would have done anything for her, even died.

I think she could even have got him to go to our village school, when it reopened in September.

But she hadn't the heart. She soon found he spoke excellent French, and they would prattle away for hours, faster than I could follow. She found he knew quite a lot of German too, but he would never speak it, even for her.

'German is language for pigs.' He also said 'Russian is language for pigs', so I suppose he had Russian as well. Neither of us could imagine him sitting at a desk among the village children.

Anyway, all his heart was set on killing Nazis. He was at the mill every spare hour. When he wasn't cleaning rifles (which he learnt quickly and did with incredible thoroughness), he was our look-out, following every vapour-trail in the sky, like a cat following the flight of birds. We found him some Home Guard overalls, nearly small enough. My mother took three inches off the leg. And we ordered him to stay at his post of duty on top of the mill, whatever happened. I think old Newsam was afraid of something nasty happening. It was the height of the Battle of Britain, and there were a lot of parachutes coming down during the daytime air-battles, and, thank God, the majority were Jerries. The farmhands of our platoon worked in the fields with their rifles at the ready. But any Jerries they rounded up, they always took straight down to the police-station in the next village. By tacit agreement, nobody ever brought a Jerry to the mill.

But Zakky certainly earned his keep. As he learnt to trust us, he would bring in the weapons from his hidden caches in the woods. Two Bren guns we returned to the Poles; Newsam gave their CO a right rocket about the security of their armoury. But the rifles we kept, and the Mills bombs and mortar-bombs. With Jerry waiting just across the Channel, we weren't inclined to be over-generous.

And at stand-to and stand-down, we would gather in amazement to hear his impromptu lectures on how to kill Nazis. He had some incredible idea about electrocuting tank-crews with the fallen electric cables from tram-cars, but as the nearest trams were fifty miles away, in Piccadilly Circus, that wasn't much good. But we liked his idea about stretching a steel cable between two tree-trunks, to decapitate Nazi despatch riders. And he showed us how to make a Molotov cocktail that really worked. And explained how to feed petrol-soaked blankets into the tracks of tanks, and how to leap on tanks from behind and block up their periscopes with a handful of mud. From the way he explained it, I thought he'd really done that. So did old Newsam.

Zakky was good for us. Half our men saw war as charging with fixed bayonets across the sea of mud and shell-holes that was no man's land. The other half saw it as slinking through the bushes, taking potshots at Jerries as if they were pheasants.

Zakky had seen tanks. In action.

But the men never loved him; he never belonged. He accepted being called 'Old Zakky' with good grace. But he would never laugh, never take part in their jokes and horseplay. Jokes were a serious waste of time. And he could never bear to be touched. Once Curly Millbank grabbed him from behind in fun and ended up on his back with a sprained wrist, which put him off work for a week.

Then came 'Cromwell'. The codeword for 'Invasion Imminent'. We shouldn't have been told, but Newsam had mates at Southern Command.

At stand-to, the men took it silently, very silently. Only Pincher Morton said, 'So it's come, then.' Some asked permission to go and say goodbye to their wives, but Newsam said no. He didn't want a panic like in France, with refugees blocking the roads. There was no argument; they were old soldiers. They got on with it.

We half blocked the London road, rolling out the great cylinders of concrete. Then all we had to do was wait, and inspect the passes of any car or lorry that passed. And watch from the top of the mill, for Jerry paratroopers landing.

I was up there with Newsam and Zakky. Below, the men who weren't manning the road-block were huddled round our transport: two private cars and a farmer's motorized haycart. The men were smoking, but cupping their hands round the glowing ends. The night was moonlit through wispy cloud. A good night for spotting parachutes. Behind our backs, London was burning again, a pulsating pink glow in the sky.

'Think we can hold them, sir?' I only said it for something to say. It felt like the start of a rugger-match against a big rugger school: not much hope of winning, but wanting to put up a good show.

'If the army can hold them on the beaches, I think we can mop up any paratroops.'

'If?' I squeaked. 'Montgomery's Third Division's down there.'

'They've got no heavy stuff; they had to leave all their heavy stuff behind at Dunkirk. Hardly an anti-tank gun to bless themselves with, poor bastards. Hardly a heavy machine-gun ...'

'So what are *we* supposed to do?'

'I expect we'd last about five minutes against tanks. But some of the men should get away into the woods. After that, it's up to them. Might as well go back to their wives; sniping won't stop an armoured column ...'

'Oh,' I said again. Was 'oh' all I could find to say?

I nodded down towards the hands cupped round cigarettes. 'Do *they* know that?'

'They know. Sorry to be a pessimist, Keith, on your first show. But I don't want you having any illusions.'

'We will kill Nazis!' said Zakky harshly, from across the observation platform. 'We will kill *many* Nazis!'

We both jumped; I think we had forgotten he was there. He came across and glared at us. I could see, in the moonlight, that he was trembling. Not with fear, I think. More like a whippet just before you unleash it against a rabbit.

'Many, many Nazis,' he said again, then went back on watch, turning his back on us. As if in disgust.

'That boy worries me,' muttered Newsam. 'Keep a tight rein on him. He's going to kill somebody before the night's out, if we're not careful. I wish we could send him home. But he'll just bugger off into the woods. Best here, where we can keep an eye on him.'

The waiting was appalling. The night was so still, except for the odd rumble or series of sharp cracks, ghosting down the warm night wind from London. The countryside I loved lay on peacefully, under the dim moon. The black bulk of the church tower. Silver light gleaming on the huddled thatch of the village. The stooks of corn in my own top field, standing neat as guards on parade. We were too far west to be in the direct path of the Jerry bombers heading for London.

Then the phone rang. A man seen climbing through the window of Elm Cottage ... Newsam shot off in his old Morris, four riflemen jammed in with him.

They were back in ten minutes. Newsam settled again, elbows on the sandbags of the parapet.

'Well?' I asked, after a long silence. I saw his shoulders heave, and thought for a wild second that he was crying. Then he said with a snort,

'Bobby Finlayson in bed with Len Taylor's missis. We dragged them both out mother-naked. There'll be hell to pay in the morning.' He couldn't stop laughing.

We were busy after that. Impounded a lorry of black market meat on its way up to London. Caught a vicar with six rover-scouts, all looking for a place to die for their country. Two courting couples in lay-bys, tanks full of black-market petrol. One enterprising burglar, with a mixed bag of silver from Mottersdon Court.

'Had no idea there was so much night-life in the country!' snorted Newsam.

*'English!'* muttered Zakky darkly to himself. But all this dashing about did everyone a bit of good. It was better than hanging around. Every time they came back they were laughing over something.

And then, just before dawn, we had three phone-calls in rapid succession, and I was left alone on top of the mill with Zakky.

Why was it then that we heard the sound of planes above the hazy moonlit clouds? And saw two parachutes sloping gently down, towards the wooded crest of Burrow's Hill, across our little valley.

While I was still dithering with shock, Zakky said 'Nazis' and was gone down the top ladder.

I suppose I should've done something intelligent, like phone for help. But I couldn't think of who to phone. Perhaps I should have run to the men manning the road-block, but they were a hundred yards away. So I stupidly left my post of duty and ran after him.

As I said before, I'd been a cross-country runner. But pound along in my hobnailed boots as I might, I couldn't catch up with Zakky. I had him in sight as far as the village, but in the cornfields beyond I lost him. I knew where the parachutes had fallen, roughly. I knew the short-cuts through the wood. But Zakky knew them even better than me ...

Yet it seemed as though I had got to a parachute first. No sign of Zakky. The chute was caught up in a tree, like a great white rustling ghost. A dark figure dangled below, about four feet off the ground, helpless, silent. I ran up to it, pulling out my dad's old Webley revolver from its First World War leather holster. I didn't know what to expect. They told us that in Holland and Belgium the German paratroops came down disguised as policemen, vicars and nuns.

But this one ... as the body swung and turned in the breeze, I saw the round top of a flying helmet and the glint on goggles. The bulk of a sheepskin flying-jacket.

'Christ,' said the body suddenly, 'cut me down, for God's sake. This crotch-strap's nearly got me cut in half.' He did sound like he was in agony. And he had a very Welsh accent.

I got out my clasp-knife and climbed the tree and cut him down somehow. I suppose it never occurred to me that a Nazi might have a Welsh accent. Anyway, once he was free, he just fell in a heap on the ground.

The next thing he said was, 'You'd better go and find Stan – Stanislav – my gunner. His English isn't much cop – he's a Pole. I don't want some yokel lynching him for a Nazi.'

'Where'd he come down?'

'Over there, somewhere.' He pointed vaguely towards the edge of the wood.

I've never run so fast in all my life. But I was too late: I found Zakky crouching over a body.

'Is dead,' said Zakky, with a lot of satisfaction.

'He's one of ours,' I said numbly, staring down at the dim white face beneath the flying-helmet. 'He was called Stanislav. He was a Pole.'

There was a long and terrifying silence. It just went on and on and on. When I couldn't stand it any longer I said,

'There's another one down the hill. He's Welsh. I think they bailed out of their night-fighter. You'd better give me a hand getting him back to the mill.'

It helped, getting the pilot down off the hill. He was quite badly hurt, and we had to carry him between us, making a chair of our hands. It gave me something to do, instead of thinking about Zakky and the dead gunner. Then I had to get the ambulance out to us.

The Welshman asked about his gunner, and I told him the gunner was dead. He just closed his eyes and nodded; I suppose they were used to losing their mates. He was a Defiant pilot, and Defiants didn't have much luck in the Battle of Britain.

Then some daft bugger over Malbury way rang the church bells, meaning the Invasion had really started, and all hell broke loose, with civilians taking to the roads, trying to get away from the coast. And then suddenly it was dawn, and word slowly trickled through that bugger-all had happened anywhere, except an extra-big raid on London.

'Ah, well,' said Newsam, 'we live to fight again.'

'Nearly time to get the cows milked,' said Pincher Morton. 'No point goin' to bed now. Just makes you feel dopey.'

I drove Zakky home. Neither of us said a word. I didn't ask him how the gunner died; I couldn't bear to know. Maybe he just found him dead. I preferred to think that. Nothing I could do would bring the gunner back to life.

They came with a hearse and took the gunner's body away, later that morning. We never heard any more about it.

Then came October, with the equinoctial gales lashing up the Channel, and news that Hitler was dispersing his flat-bottomed barges at Boulogne. We were safe for the winter.

Newsam still drove us hard. He talked endlessly about *when* Hitler came in the spring. We trained more men; we were a full company now, four platoons, and I was a platoon-commander. They built us pill-boxes of foot-thick concrete, and we trained with something called a Blacker Bombard that threw thermite-bombs at fake tanks made of corrugated iron which ran down a little railway outside Eastbourne. But somehow we couldn't *quite* believe in it; there was a feeling that Hitler had missed the boat.

All except Zakky, who grew grimmer than ever. He made this huge plywood cut-out of a Nazi storm-trooper, advancing with a hideous grimace and a sub-machine-gun. Spent hours throwing his knife at it. I'd never believed in throwing-knives, couldn't see how they could even go through the cloth of a uniform. They were something you saw in the movies. But

Zakky could throw from all angles and never missed, and I once tried levering his knife out of the thick plywood. It was embedded two inches, and I had a hell of a time getting it out. One or two of the platoon had narrow squeaks, coming across Zakky without warning when he was practising. It didn't make him any more loved. But he was something to talk about in the dull times, when we were out all night in the rain, and had nothing to show for it but the crew of some Jerry night-bomber, well soaked and ready to surrender for a mug of tea.

But we had to find him something to do, besides endlessly oiling rifles and throwing his knife at plywood. My mother got more and more worried about him. And the rabbits he brought back from the woods, always killed by his knife, did nothing to lessen her worries, though they helped out the rations.

Then came the blessed day that my new Fordson tractor broke down, only a week out of the factory. Furious, I rang Tom Hands the blacksmith, who fiddled with cars as a sideline.

That evening, when I got back from ploughing with our two old horses, the tractor was mended, and Tom and Zakky were in the kitchen with my mother, drinking tea from white enamel mugs, smirched with oily fingerprints. They were all as thick as thieves.

Tom announced that Zakky had a gift with engines. My mother announced that Tom was taking on Zakky as an apprentice. As spring broadened into summer, Tom and Zakky became inseparable. Worn-out farm machinery kept breaking down all over the place; they never had an idle moment.

And then Hitler invaded Russia, and we knew the threat from across the Channel was gone. To celebrate, Pincher Morton bought himself a plot in the village churchyard. Said he felt happier, knowing where he was going to end up.

We all felt happier; except Zakky. The further away the threat of invasion got, the blacker he became. You could feel the pressure building up in him. He was always wanting to *wrestle* with me. I took him on once or twice, in fun. Going gently, not wanting to hurt him, for I was a big lad by then, nearly fourteen stone.

He had me on my face in about ten seconds; somebody had taught him unarmed combat along the way. He never hurt me, but it was bloody humiliating. In the end I refused to do it any more, so he began jumping out on me from dark corners. Said I had to learn, for when the Nazis came.

But it wasn't the Nazis who came; it was the Canadians, whole divisions of them, armed to the teeth with American tanks and guns and lorries.

We had to pretend to defend the villages, while the Canadians pretended to attack them. Quite realistic, it was. Blank ammunition, thunderflashes, wired explosions, smoke-grenades. The trouble was, we were pretty good by then, and we knew the countryside. And they were so *green*; lousy soldiers who bunched up too close together, and stuck to the metalled roads. We ambushed and slaughtered them over and over again. Then they gave us fags and chewing-gum, grinning sheepishly. The battle-umpires kept running up and telling us *we* were dead, without giving any reasons. I don't think they wanted the Canadians to get too discouraged. Our old hands weren't too surprised when the Canadians finally got a bloody nose from real Germans, in the Dieppe Raid.

It was from one of these exercises that Zakky didn't come home. My mother and I were just setting out to look for him, in the van, when word came that Zakky was being held by the military. It seemed he had gone berserk and seriously injured a Canadian ...

Major Newsam drove up to London, with my mother and the vicar. They must have talked bloody hard, because they brought Zakky back with them, paler and more silent, and blacker in his moods than ever.

Some weeks later, as we were getting ready for Christmas, the Japs attacked Pearl Harbor. In the New

Year, we settled down to teaching the first American troops a thing or two.

All except Zakky.

The Americans were even more generous and clumsy than the Canadians had been. But, as Major Newsam said sadly, when we got our first issue of American tommy-guns, us Home Guard were all dressed up with nowhere to go. We were just actors now; the invasion threat had gone for ever. Still, we enjoyed the Camels and Hershey Bars.

Zakky was sixteen by then; as tall as he ever got, five feet seven. He shaved earlier than me, had a fine black moustache, whereas I could still get away with shaving twice a week. I suppose he was handsome in a thin, peaky, tragic sort of way. A lot of the local girls eyed him, even with the Americans about. Rosemary Thomas, whose dad ran the White Lion, especially, though she was older than he was. I suppose the girls sensed the darkness in him; wanted to rescue him from it. But he had little time for them ...

He was well in with the local farmers too. A natural mechanic, which was quite something in those days when we had to hold tractors together with tin cans and wire. I know he brought my mother's car back from the grave more than once, though he always insisted afterwards that she crawl underneath it, to be shown exactly what he'd done. He'd still do anything for her.

He even talked German now. Because she'd hit on a way of holding him steady. Soon, she told him, a great army would be invading Europe to fight the Nazis. They would need people who could speak French and German fluently ... I think Major Newsam had something to do with that. He and my mother were as thick as thieves by that time. But I wasn't jealous. It was just nice to see two people I liked being happy.

They got married after harvest. October 1943. The whole village nearly went mad over it. We'd had a lot of wartime weddings, with blokes going off to the war, and people thinking they wouldn't come back. Desperate weddings, a kind of laughter on the edge of the grave. But my mother's wedding was different. It was, in a way, the first of our post-war weddings. People knew *they* were going to stay around and be married for the rest of their natural lives. There was no desperation in the laughter. We held the reception in the village hall, and the whole neighbourhood made a festival of it. They were both pretty popular with the locals and everyone chipped in with the eats, so we had a good spread in spite of the rationing. I gave my mother away in church and made a speech afterwards, which got a lot of laughs, Major Newsam being older than me, and my commanding officer in the Home Guard, which gave me plenty of openings for funny cracks.

I still have a photo of Zakky taken at the reception. My mother had asked him to be a groomsman, and he looked very dashing in hired morning-dress, holding his glass and laughing. He was willing to be happy for my mother, when he would never be happy for himself. And behind him in the photo is Rosemary Thomas, looking at him as if she wanted to eat him. Even now, when I look at it, it makes me shudder.

That Christmas Zakky got his chance. Major Newsam took him up for an interview at the War Office, and apparently he chattered French and English and German and Polish like a bird, and they grabbed him like he was the best thing since sliced bread.

He came back for a fortnight's leave in May 1944, in the uniform of the Intelligence Corps. He was truly happy, I think, for that fortnight. Southern England was, by that time, as packed with allied soldiers as an egg is full of meat, and he knew at last he was going to have his feast of death. He wasn't even eighteen, but he'd have passed for twenty-five with his hair cropped.

We went for a last walk before he left. My bottom field was full of Shermans under camouflage, and the

Yank tank-crews bivouacked. He was quickly among them, shaking hands and laughing and talking about killing Nazis. It was pretty crazy and pretty painful, because the Yanks kept looking at each other and tapping their heads with their fingers, once he'd passed. I was bloody terrified he'd see them, because the little bulge at the back of his battle-dress collar told me the deadly knife was still there.

Walking home, we met Rosemary Thomas in the lane outside our house. I think she'd come looking for him. They went off together, his arm around her waist, natural as any young couple, laughing.

But I shuddered. He could afford to laugh, because he was going to kill. He could afford to love, because he was going to die. He was like a dragonfly that only lives a few days of summer; a dragonfly that is a gaudy killer.

I thought of him on D-Day. D-Day was a strange time for us Home Guard. Endless streams of allied planes flying east, where once there had been endless streams of Germans flying west. Endless streams of American armour pouring through our village, where once we'd stood expecting streams of German panzers.

In one day we became pointless. No one left to fight; no one even left to train. Our hands full of the very latest, useless guns. Newsam told me an order was coming out, to disband us, with thanks. We'd never fired a shot in anger; only blanks at friends.

Still, there was the harvest to get in. The hay was early that year. And that night I first met Shirley Harris, as we gathered round the radio in the pub to listen to the news from Normandy.

He never wrote.

There was one snippet about him in the local paper. BIRSBY MAN WINS MILITARY MEDAL.

Major Newsam tried to find out more from his mates at the War Office. He got very little, except that Zakky had been promoted to sergeant. And a hint of cloak-and-dagger. Raids behind enemy lines, co-operation with the French Maquis, throats cut and no questions asked. A very dirty war indeed.

'Not my kind of war,' said Newsam. 'Not my kind of war at all.'

And then, nothing. VE day passed with great rejoicing, our village green packed with trestle tables, hung with red, white and blue bunting left over from the Coronation, the Silver Jubilee, Queen Victoria's birthday, for all I knew. We choked with the dust as we hung it up. A little band played for dancing, and women danced with women and children. Then VJ day, and the men began coming home, and still nothing. Six weeks later I married Shirley Harris. There was nothing to stop us. My mother had gone to live with the Major, in a country club he was trying to haul back to life further along the south coast.

And then, towards the back-end of 1945, I got home from a cattle auction, and Shirley met me in the yard and said,

'You've got a visitor.'

She looked scared to death, and she's not the nervous sort. So I went in feeling very proprietorial, and rather angry.

He was sitting at the kitchen table. Shirley had given him a cup of tea and a piece of home-made cake, as she did with everybody who called. He'd let the tea go cold, and rolled her good cake into tiny dark balls on the plate. Our kitchen was full of ... the smell of him? The *vibes* of him? The only thing I can compare it to was the atmosphere at the funeral of a friend who had committed suicide. It was that black.

I made myself shake hands. His hand was very bony and cold. His hair was cropped like a convict's; you could see the white scalp showing through the black stubble. His flamboyant moustache was gone. So was any glint of life in his eyes; they were like two holes burnt in a grey blanket.

I said I was glad to see him, but I wasn't. I asked him whether he'd been demobbed. He said,

'They have stopped killing Nazis. Germany is full of Nazis but they are making them into burgomasters now. Because they are the only ones left who can run that country.' I noticed he was wearing one of those awful demob suits; it hung on him as it might have hung on a rail.

I tried to tell him about this and that; country gossip. But he cut me short, he didn't want to know.

I told myself he was still only a kid, not yet nineteen. But he wasn't. I even began to wish he had died, like the dragonfly, that gaudy killer. So that he didn't have to come back here and plague us. I began to worry he might ask after my mother ...

In the end I said, straight out,

'What can I do for you, Zakky?'

'I wish to rent the mill. I will pay you fair rent.'

Should I have said no? So he might have drifted off and plagued somebody else? But all I wanted was him out of my kitchen, and the mill seemed a cheap price to pay. It still had its floors and roof, as the Home Guard had left it. I had no use for it.

We agreed a rent. I wasn't such a fool as to offer it to him for nothing, but I threw in some old furniture. Anything to get him out of my kitchen. He was death, walking. They had glutted him with killing, then turned him loose on a world at peace.

And yet, it might still have worked for him. Lost in the world as he was, the mill became his fortress, the one place where his life had meaning. He kept it spotless, I was told. He even filled the little walled enclosure full of flowers. Only all the colours were those of the old Polish flag. A Polish flag now flew from the little flagpole we'd left on the roof. Inside, there was another Polish flag, draped round a photograph of the late General Sikorski. And there was a large radio, permanently tuned to Radio Warsaw.

But Poland was Communist now; full of Russians talking the language of pigs. We all knew he could never go home.

He scratched a living, mending machinery. Tom Hands offered him a partnership, but he refused. You never saw him talking to anybody round the village. But when he met any member of the old Home Guard, he would give a curt, abrupt nod of the head.

Only Rosemary Thomas did not despair. She beat against the walls of that mill, like a moth beating against a lamp. But, it seemed, in vain.

Yet she found fresh-killed rabbits on the pub doorstep some mornings. Killed by a knife-throw.

And then PC Morris from the next village came to

see me. He'd heard rumours that Zakky had guns hung on the wall. Not shotguns, either. Guns from the war, people said ...

I told him it was rubbish. They *must* be shotguns. I said I would be responsible for Zakky; see he didn't cause any trouble. Frankly, I told him anything I could think of, to get him to go away.

To tell the truth, I feared for his life, if he tried to interfere.

And then, God help us, came the start of the post-war housing boom. Homes fit for heroes. Town vied with town. And our blessed district council decided to double the size of our village. On my land. By compulsory purchase order.

Mind you, they offered a fair price, and I had my eye on a bigger farm. I had no cause to grumble.

Till I heard the mill had to go, too.

I *pleaded* with the clerk to the council. I spent four hours trying to explain about Zakky. Didn't make a ha'p'orth of difference. Even ex-servicemen with valiant war-records must learn to make way for progress. Why, this whole scheme was *designed* for ex-servicemen. Mr Zakrewski might apply for one of the houses, if he was a married man with at least two children. But if he insisted on being awkward, that was surely a matter for the police ...

Truly, I felt the ground open up beneath me.

I was still moving in that dark nightmare the following morning when I drove my tractor on to a too-steep bit of hillside, and it turned over on me. I was in a coma for six weeks, and my life was despaired of.

The morning Shirley finally drove me home from hospital, we came in on the road past Draggett's Mill.

It was gone; flat. All around, workmen were digging foundations for houses.

'Zakky ...' I said. Full of dread, loss, a terrible feeling of letting people down.

'Gone,' said Shirley. 'Safe gone.'

'HOW?'

'Birsby Home Guard's last and best manoeuvre ...'

'What *sort* of manoeuvre?'

'Old Comrades' Reunion. At Rosemary's pub. Zakky was formally requested to attend, or his old comrades would be *deeply* insulted. Given that Polish sense of honour, could Zakky refuse? Just for half an hour of course ...'

'And then ...?'

'Well, people began to drink toasts, with vodka bought off a Polish ship in Southampton. Oh, so *many* toasts. The late General Sikorski, and every member of his late government. Major Newsam had all their names off by heart, and nearly cracked his jaw pronouncing them. Zakky kept correcting him.

Then Mr Churchill, President Roosevelt, President Truman, Chang Kai-Shek, General de Gaulle, the RAF, the Home Guard, the Royal Navy. You name it, we had it. And Zakky couldn't refuse to drink to a single one, could he? On his Polish honour. And he was drinking neat vodka, and the rest were drinking vodka and water. Half the pub's glasses ended up smashed at the back of the pub fireplace. And every time a vodka glass was smashed, the flames would leap up nearly to the pub ceiling. A right little fire risk. Zakky loved every moment of it. Till he passed out cold.'

'Then?'

'Well, they had to carry him home to the mill, didn't they? And they took the rest of the vodka with them. And he'd left a fire burning at the mill. And ... or so they said ... they started drinking again, and smashing more glasses in the fireplace in true Polish fashion, and a full bottle of vodka somehow got broken in the fireplace, and ... well, the whole mill went up in flames, and they only just got Zakky out in time. The mill was alight from top to bottom by the time the fire brigade got there. Weapons, bullets, hand-grenades, the lot went up. Quite a little fireworks display. There wasn't a lot left of the mill by the time they were finished. Even the stone walls fell in.'

'How did Zakky take it?'

'Well, they'd carried him back to the pub, overnight.

And Rosemary was fluttering about him, tending to his hangover. And they all looked very sheepish, and told him what they'd done, and how sorry they were. And that they felt honour-bound to make amends for his loss.

And he could hardly blame them for going on in such a Polish way, could he? Nor refuse their honourable desire to make amends. He went off with five hundred quid in his pocket. I think Major Newsam gave half ...'

'What good is *money* to him?' I asked desperately.

'Oh, I wouldn't worry too much about him. Rosemary went with him.'

'Where, for God's sake?'

'Marbury, in Cheshire, according to Rosemary's letters. Hundreds of ex-Polish army up there. Starting to marry local girls, thinking of building their own church. She still has hopes he'll do the honourable thing, and marry her. Of course, she had a hand in the whole thing from the start ...'

'*Women*,' I said.

'Women,' she agreed, smiling. 'What would you all do without us? Welcome home, Keith.'

# THE DESTRUCTORS

## Graham Greene

**1**

It was on the eve of August Bank Holiday that the latest recruit became the leader of the Wormsley Common Gang. No one was surprised except Mike, but Mike at the age of nine was surprised by everything. 'If you don't shut your mouth,' somebody once said to him, 'you'll get a frog down it.' After that Mike kept his teeth tightly clamped except when the surprise was too great.

The new recruit had been with the gang since the beginning of the summer holidays, and there were possibilities about his brooding silence that all recognized. He never wasted a word even to tell his name until that was required of him by the rules. When he said 'Trevor' it was a statement of fact, not as it would have been with the others a statement of shame or defiance. Nor did anyone laugh except Mike, who finding himself without support and meeting the dark gaze of the newcomer opened his mouth and was quiet again. There was every reason why T., as he was afterwards referred to, should have been an object of mockery – there was his name (and they substituted the initial because otherwise they had no excuse not to laugh at it), the fact that his father, a former architect and present clerk, had 'come down in the world' and that his mother considered herself better than the neighbours. What but an odd quality of danger, of the unpredictable, established him in the gang without any ignoble ceremony of initiation?

The gang met every morning in an impromptu car-park, the site of the last bomb of the first blitz. The leader, who was known as Blackie, claimed to have heard it fall, and no one was precise enough in his dates to point out that he would have been one year old and fast asleep on the down platform of Wormsley Common Underground Station. On one side of the car-park leant the first occupied house, No. 3, of the shattered Northwood Terrace – literally leant, for it had suffered from the blast of the bomb and the side walls were supported on wooden struts. A smaller bomb and incendiaries had fallen beyond, so that the house stuck up like a jagged tooth and carried on the further wall relics of its neighbour, a dado, the remains of a fireplace. T., whose words were almost confined to voting 'Yes' or 'No' to the plan of operations proposed each day by Blackie, once startled the whole gang by saying broodingly, 'Wren built that house, father says.'

'Who's Wren?'

'The man who built St Paul's.'

'Who cares?' Blackie said. 'It's only Old Misery's.'

Old Misery – whose real name was Thomas – had once been a builder and decorator. He lived alone in the crippled house, doing for himself: once a week you could see him coming back across the common with bread and vegetables, and once as the boys played in the car-park he put his head over the smashed wall of his garden and looked at them.

'Been to the lav,' one of the boys said, for it was common knowledge that since the bombs fell something had gone wrong with the pipes of the house and Old Misery was too mean to spend money on the property. He could do the redecorating himself at cost price, but he had never learnt plumbing. The lav was a wooden shed at the bottom of the narrow garden with a star-shaped hole in the door: it had escaped the blast which had smashed the house next door and sucked out the window-frames of No. 3.

The next time the gang became aware of Mr Thomas was more surprising. Blackie, Mike and a thin yellow boy, who for some reason was called by his surname Summers, met him on the common coming back from the market. Mr Thomas stopped them. He said glumly, 'You belong to the lot that play in the car-park?'

Mike was about to answer when Blackie stopped him. As the leader he had responsibilities. 'Suppose we are?' he said ambiguously.

'I got some chocolates,' Mr Thomas said. 'Don't like 'em myself. Here you are. Not enough to go round, I don't suppose.

'There never is,' he added with sombre conviction. He handed over three packets of Smarties.

The gang was puzzled and perturbed by this action and tried to explain it away. 'Bet someone dropped them and he picked 'em up,' somebody suggested.

'Pinched 'em and then got in a bleeding funk,' another thought aloud.

'It's a bribe,' Summers said. 'He wants us to stop bouncing balls on his wall.'

'We'll show him we don't take bribes,' Blackie said, and they sacrificed the whole morning to the game of bouncing that only Mike was young enough to enjoy. There was no sign from Mr Thomas.

Next day T. astonished them all. He was late at the rendezvous, and the voting for that day's exploit took place without him. At Blackie's suggestion the gang was to disperse in pairs, take buses at random and see how many free rides could be snatched from unwary conductors (the operation was to be carried out in pairs to avoid cheating). They were drawing lots for their companions when T. arrived.

'Where you been, T.?' Blackie asked. 'You can't vote now. You know the rules.'

'I've been *there*,' T. said. He looked at the ground, as though he had thoughts to hide.

'Where?'

'At Old Misery's.' Mike's mouth opened and then hurriedly closed again with a click. He had remembered the frog.

'At Old Misery's?' Blackie said. There was nothing in the rules against it, but he had a sensation that T. was treading on dangerous ground. He asked hopefully, 'Did you break in?'

'No. I rang the bell.'

'And what did you say?'

'I said I wanted to see his house.'

'What did he do?'

'He showed it me.'

'Pinch anything?'

'No.'

'What did you do it for then?'

The gang had gathered round: it was as though an impromptu court were about to form and try some case of deviation. T. said, 'It's a beautiful house,' and still watching the ground, meeting no one's eyes, he licked his lips first one way, then the other.

'What do you mean, a beautiful house?' Blackie asked with scorn.

'It's got a staircase two hundred years old like a corkscrew. Nothing holds it up.'

'What do you mean, nothing holds it up. Does it float?'

'It's to do with opposite forces, Old Misery said.'

'What else?'

'There's panelling.'

'Like in the Blue Boar?'

'Two hundred years old.'

'Is Old Misery two hundred years old?'

Mike laughed suddenly and then was quiet again. The meeting was in a serious mood. For the first time since T. had strolled into the car-park on the first day of the holidays his position was in danger. It only needed a single use of his real name and the gang would be at his heels.

'What did you do it for?' Blackie asked. He was just, he had no jealousy, he was anxious to retain T. in the gang if he could. It was the word 'beautiful' that worried him – that belonged to a class world that you could still see parodied at the Wormsley Common Empire by a man wearing a top hat and a monocle, with a haw-haw accent. He was tempted to say, 'My dear Trevor, old chap,' and unleash his hell hounds. 'If you'd broken in,' he said sadly – that indeed would have been an exploit worthy of the gang.

'This was better,' T. said. 'I found out things.' He continued to stare at his feet, not meeting anybody's eye, as though he were absorbed in some dream he was unwilling – or ashamed – to share.

'What things?'

'Old Misery's going to be away all tomorrow and Bank Holiday.'

Blackie said with relief, 'You mean we could break in?'

'And pinch things?' somebody asked.

Blackie said, 'Nobody's going to pinch things. Breaking in – that's good enough, isn't it? We don't want any court stuff.'

'I don't want to pinch anything,' T. said. 'I've got a better idea.'

'What is it?'

T. raised eyes, as grey and disturbed as the drab August day. 'We'll pull it down,' he said. 'We'll destroy it.'

Blackie gave a single hoot of laughter and then, like Mike, fell quiet, daunted by the serious implacable gaze. 'What'd the police be doing all the time?' he said.

'They'd never know. We'd do it from inside. I've found a way in.' He said with a sort of intensity, 'We'd be like worms, don't you see, in an apple. When we came out again there'd be nothing there, no staircase, no panels, nothing but just walls, and then we'd make the walls fall down – somehow.'

'We'd go to jug,' Blackie said.

'Who's to prove? and anyway we wouldn't have pinched anything.' He added without the smallest flicker of glee, 'There wouldn't be anything to pinch after we'd finished.'

'I've never heard of going to prison for breaking things,' Summers said.

'There wouldn't be time,' Blackie said. 'I've seen housebreakers at work.'

'There are twelve of us,' T. said. 'We'd organize.'

'None of us know how …'

'I know,' T. said. He looked across at Blackie. 'Have you got a better plan?'

'Today,' Mike said tactlessly, 'we're pinching free rides …'

'Free rides,' T. said. 'Kid stuff. You can stand down, Blackie, if you'd rather …'

'The gang's got to vote.'

'Put it up then.'

Blackie said uneasily, 'It's proposed that tomorrow and Monday we destroy Old Misery's house.'

'Here, here,' said a fat boy called Joe.

'Who's in favour?'

T. said, 'It's carried.'

'How do we start?' Summers asked.

'He'll tell you,' Blackie said. It was the end of his leadership. He went away to the back of the car-park and began to kick a stone, dribbling it this way and that. There was only one old Morris in the park, for few cars were left there except lorries: without an attendant there was no safety. He took a flying kick at the car and scraped a little paint off the rear mudguard. Beyond, paying no more attention to him than to a stranger, the gang had gathered round T.; Blackie was dimly aware of the fickleness of favour. He thought of going home, of never returning, of letting them all discover the hollowness of T.'s leadership, but suppose after all what T. proposed was possible – nothing like it had ever been done before. The fame of the Wormsley Common car-park gang would surely reach around London. There would be headlines in the papers. Even the grown-up gangs who ran the betting at the all-in wrestling and the barrow-boys would hear with respect of how Old Misery's house had been destroyed. Driven by the pure, simple and altruistic ambition of fame for the gang, Blackie came back to where T. stood in the shadow of Old Misery's wall.

T. was giving his orders with decision: it was as though this plan had been with him all his life, pondered through the seasons, now in his fifteenth year crystallized with the pain of puberty. 'You,' he said to Mike, 'bring some big nails, the biggest you can find, and a hammer. Anybody who can, better bring a hammer and a screwdriver. We'll need plenty of them. Chisels too. We can't have too many chisels. Can anybody bring a saw?'

'I can,' Mike said.

'Not a child's saw,' T. said. 'A real saw.'

Blackie realized he had raised his hand like any ordinary member of the gang.

'Right, you bring one, Blackie. But now there's a difficulty. We want a hacksaw.'

'What's a hacksaw?' someone asked.

'You can get 'em at Woolworth's,' Summers said.

The fat boy called Joe said gloomily, 'I knew it would end in a collection.'

'I'll get one myself,' T. said. 'I don't want your money. But I can't buy a sledge-hammer.'

Blackie said, 'They are working on No. 15. I know where they'll leave their stuff for Bank Holiday.'

'Then that's all,' T. said. 'We meet here at nine sharp.'

'I've got to go to church,' Mike said.

'Come over the wall and whistle. We'll let you in.'

## 2

On Sunday morning all were punctual except Blackie, even Mike. Mike had a stroke of luck. His mother felt ill, his father was tired after Saturday night, and he was told to go to church alone with many warnings of what would happen if he strayed. Blackie had difficulty in smuggling out the saw, and then in finding the sledge-hammer at the back of No. 15. He approached the house from a lane at the rear of the garden, for fear of the policeman's beat along the main road. The tired evergreens kept off a stormy sun: another wet Bank Holiday was being prepared over the Atlantic, beginning in swirls of dust under the trees. Blackie climbed the wall into Misery's garden.

There was no sign of anybody anywhere. The lav stood like a tomb in a neglected graveyard. The curtains were drawn. The house slept. Blackie lumbered nearer with the saw and the sledge-hammer. Perhaps after all nobody had turned up: the plan had been a wild invention: they had woken wiser. But when he came close to the back door he could hear a confusion of sound hardly louder than a hive in swarm: a clickety-clack, a bang bang, a scraping, a creaking, a sudden painful crack. He thought: it's true, and whistled.

They opened the back door to him and he came in. He had at once the impression of organization, very different from the old happy-go-lucky ways under his leadership. For a while he wandered up and down stairs looking for T. Nobody addressed him: he had a sense of great urgency, and already he could begin to see the plan. The interior of the house was being carefully demolished without touching the walls. Summers with hammer and chisel was ripping out the skirting-boards in the ground floor dining-room: he had already smashed the panels of the door. In the same room Joe was heaving up the parquet blocks, exposing the soft wood floorboards over the cellar. Coils of wire came out of the damaged skirting and Mike sat happily on the floor clipping the wires.

On the curved stairs two of the gang were working hard with an inadequate child's saw on the banisters – when they saw Blackie's big saw they signalled for it wordlessly. When he next saw them a quarter of the banisters had been dropped into the hall. He found T. at last in the bathroom – he sat moodily in the least cared-for room in the house, listening to the sounds coming up from below.

'You've really done it,' Blackie said with awe. 'What's going to happen?'

'We've only just begun,' T. said. He looked at the sledge-hammer and gave his instructions. 'You stay here and break the bath and the wash-basin. Don't bother about the pipes. They come later.'

Mike appeared at the door. 'I've finished the wires, T.,' he said.

'Good. You've just got to go wandering round now. The kitchen's in the basement. Smash all the china and glass and bottles you can lay hold of. Don't turn on the taps – we don't want a flood – yet. Then go into all the rooms and turn out the drawers. If they are locked get one of the others to break them open. Tear up any papers you find and smash all the ornaments. Better take a carving knife with you from the kitchen. The bedroom's opposite here. Open the pillows and tear up the sheets. That's enough for the moment. And you, Blackie, when you've finished in here crack the plaster in the passage up with your sledge-hammer.'

'What are you going to do?' Blackie asked.

'I'm looking for something special,' T. said.

It was nearly lunch-time before Blackie had finished and went in search of T. Chaos had advanced. The kitchen was a shambles of broken glass and china. The dining-room was stripped of parquet, the skirting was up, the door had been taken off its hinges, and the destroyers had moved up a floor. Streaks of light came in through the closed shutters where they worked with the seriousness of creators - and destruction after all is a form of creation. A kind of imagination had seen this house as it had now become.

Mike said, 'I've got to go home for dinner.'

'Who else?' T. asked, but all the others on one excuse or another had brought provisions with them.

They squatted in the ruins of the room and swapped unwanted sandwiches. Half an hour for lunch and they were at work again. By the time Mike returned they were on the top floor, and by six the superficial damage was completed. The doors were all off, all the skirtings raised, the furniture pillaged and ripped and smashed – no one could have slept in the house except on a bed of broken plaster. T. gave his orders – eight o'clock next morning, and to escape notice they climbed singly over the garden wall, into the car-park. Only Blackie and T. were left: the light had nearly gone, and when they touched a switch, nothing worked – Mike had done his job thoroughly.

'Did you find anything special?' Blackie asked.

T. nodded. 'Come over here,' he said, 'and look.' Out of both pockets he drew bundles of pound notes. 'Old Misery's savings,' he said. 'Mike ripped out the mattress, but he missed them.'

'What are you going to do? Share them?'

'We aren't thieves,' T. said. 'Nobody's going to steal anything from this house. I kept these for you and me – a celebration.' He knelt down on the floor and counted them out – there were seventy in all. 'We'll burn them,' he said, 'one by one,' and taking it in turns they held a note upwards and lit the top corner, so that the flame burnt slowly towards their fingers. The grey ash floated above them and fell on their heads like age. 'I'd like to see Old Misery's face when we are through,' T. said.

'You hate him a lot?' Blackie asked.

'Of course I don't hate him,' T. said. 'There'd be no fun if I hated him.' The last burning note illuminated his brooding face. 'All this hate and love,' he said, 'it's soft, it's hooey. There's only things, Blackie,' and he looked round the room crowded with the unfamiliar shadows of half things, broken things, former things. 'I'll race you home, Blackie,' he said.

## 3

Next morning the serious destruction started. Two were missing – Mike and another boy whose parents were off to Southend and Brighton in spite of the slow warm drops that had begun to fall and the rumble of thunder in the estuary like the first guns of the old blitz. 'We've got to hurry,' T. said.

Summers was restive. 'Haven't we done enough?' he asked. 'I've been given a bob for slot machines. This is like work.'

'We've hardly started,' T. said. 'Why, there's all the floors left, and the stairs. We haven't taken out a single window. You voted like the others. We are going to *destroy* this house. There won't be anything left when we've finished.'

They began again on the first floor picking up the

top floorboards next to the outer wall, leaving the joists exposed. Then they sawed through the joists and retreated into the hall, as what was left of the floor heeled and sank. They had learnt with practice, and the second floor collapsed more easily. By the evening an odd exhilaration seized them as they looked down the great hollow of the house. They ran risks and made mistakes: when they thought of the windows it was too late to reach them. 'Cor,' Joe said, and dropped a penny down into the dry rubble-filled well. It cracked and span amongst the broken glass.

'Why did we start this?' Summers asked with astonishment; T. was already on the ground, digging at the rubble, clearing a space along the outer wall. 'Turn on the taps,' he said. 'It's too dark for anyone to see now, and in the morning it won't matter.' The water overtook them on the stairs and fell through the floorless rooms.

It was then they heard Mike's whistle at the back. 'Something's wrong,' Blackie said. They could hear his urgent breathing as they unlocked the door.

'The bogies?' Summers asked.

'Old Misery,' Mike said. 'He's on his way,' he said with pride.

'But why?' T. said. 'He told me ...' He protested with the fury of the child he had never been, 'It isn't fair.'

'He was down at Southend,' Mike said, 'and he was on the train coming back. Said it was too cold and wet.' He paused and gazed at the water. 'My, you've had a storm here. Is the roof leaking?'

'How long will he be?'

'Five minutes. I gave Ma the slip and ran.'

'We better clear,' Summers said. 'We've done enough, anyway.'

'Oh no, we haven't. Anybody could do this –' 'this' was the shattered hollowed house with nothing left but the walls. Yet walls could be preserved. Façades were valuable. They could build inside again more beautifully than before. This could again be a home. He said angrily, 'We've got to finish. Don't move. Let me think.'

'There's no time,' a boy said.

'There's got to be a way,' T. said. 'We couldn't have got this far ...'

'We've done a lot,' Blackie said.

'No. No, we haven't. Somebody watch the front.'

'We can't do any more.'

'He may come in at the back.'

'Watch the back too.' T. began to plead. 'Just give me a minute and I'll fix it. I swear I'll fix it.' But his authority had gone with his ambiguity. He was only one of the gang. 'Please,' he said.

'Please,' Summers mimicked him, and then suddenly

struck home with the fatal name. 'Run along home, Trevor.'

T. stood with his back to the rubble like a boxer knocked groggy against the ropes. He had no words as his dreams shook and slid. Then Blackie acted before the gang had time to laugh, pushing Summers backward. 'I'll watch the front, T.,' he said, and cautiously he opened the shutters of the hall. The grey wet common stretched ahead, and the lamps gleamed in the puddles. 'Someone's coming, T. No, it's not him. What's your plan, T.?'

'Tell Mike to go out to the lav and hide close beside it. When he hears me whistle he's got to count ten and start to shout.'

'Shout what?'

'Oh, "Help", anything.'

'You hear, Mike,' Blackie said. He was the leader again. He took a quick look between the shutters. 'He's coming, T.'

'Quick, Mike. The lav. Stay here, Blackie, all of you, till I yell.'

'Where are you going, T.?'

'Don't worry. I'll see to this. I said I would, didn't I?'

Old Misery came limping off the common. He had mud on his shoes and he stopped to scrape them on the pavement's edge. He didn't want to soil his house, which stood jagged and dark between the bomb-sites, saved so narrowly, as he believed, from destruction. Even the fan-light had been left unbroken by the bomb's blast. Somewhere somebody whistled. Old Misery looked sharply round. He didn't trust whistles. A child was shouting: it seemed to come from his own garden. Then a boy ran into the road from the car-park. 'Mr Thomas,' he called, 'Mr Thomas.'

'What is it?'

'I'm terribly sorry, Mr Thomas. One of us got taken short, and we thought you wouldn't mind, and now he can't get out.'

'What do you mean, boy?'

'He's got stuck in your lav.'

'He'd no business ... Haven't I seen you before?'

'You showed me your house.'

'So I did. So I did. That doesn't give you the right to ...'

'Do hurry, Mr Thomas. He'll suffocate.'

'Nonsense. He can't suffocate. Wait till I put my bag in.'

'I'll carry your bag.'

'Oh no, you don't. I carry my own.'

'This way, Mr Thomas.'

'I can't get in the garden that way. I've got to go through the house.'

'But you *can* get in the garden this way, Mr Thomas. We often do.'

'You often do?' He followed the boy with a scandalized fascination.

'When? What right ... ?'

'Do you see ... ? the wall's low.'

'I'm not going to climb walls into my own garden. It's absurd.'

'This is how we do it. One foot here, one foot there, and over.' The boy's face peered down, an arm shot out, and Mr Thomas found his bag taken and deposited on the other side of the wall.

'Give me back my bag,' Mr Thomas said. From the loo a boy yelled and yelled. 'I'll call the police.'

'Your bag's all right, Mr Thomas. Look. One foot there. On your right. Now just above. To your left.' Mr Thomas climbed over his own garden wall. 'Here's your bag, Mr Thomas.'

'I'll have the wall built up,' Mr Thomas said, 'I'll not have you boys coming over here, using my loo.' He stumbled on the path, but the boy caught his elbow and supported him. 'Thank you, thank you, my boy,' he murmured automatically. Somebody shouted again through the dark. 'I'm coming, I'm coming,' Mr Thomas called. He said to the boy beside him, 'I'm not unreasonable. Been a boy myself. As long as things are done regular. I don't mind you playing round the place Saturday mornings. Sometimes I like company. Only it's got to be regular. One of you asks leave and I say Yes.

Sometimes I'll say No. Won't feel like it. And you come in at the front door and out at the back. No garden walls.'

'Do get him out, Mr Thomas.'

'He won't come to any harm in my loo,' Mr Thomas said, stumbling slowly down the garden. 'Oh, my rheumatics,' he said. 'Always get 'em on Bank Holiday. I've got to be careful. There's loose stones here. Give me your hand. Do you know what my horoscope said yesterday? "Abstain from any dealings in first half of week. Danger of serious crash." That might be on this path,' Mr Thomas said. 'They speak in parables and double meanings.' He paused at the door of the loo. 'What's the matter in there?' he called. There was no reply.

'Perhaps he's fainted,' the boy said.

'Not in my loo. Here, you, come out,' Mr Thomas said, and giving a great jerk at the door he nearly fell on his back when it swung easily open. A hand first supported him and then pushed him hard. His head hit the opposite wall and he sat heavily down. His bag hit his feet. A hand whipped the key out of the lock and the door slammed. 'Let me out,' he called, and heard the key turn in the lock. 'A serious crash,' he thought, and felt dithery and confused and old.

A voice spoke to him softly through the star-shaped hole in the door. 'Don't worry, Mr Thomas,' it said, 'we won't hurt you, not if you stay quiet.'

Mr Thomas put his head between his hands and pondered. He had noticed that there was only one lorry in the car-park, and he felt certain that the driver would not come for it before the morning. Nobody could hear him from the road in front, and the lane at the back was seldom used. Anyone who passed there would be hurrying home and would not pause for what they would certainly take to be drunken cries. And if he did call 'Help', who, on a lonely Bank Holiday evening, would have the courage to investigate? Mr Thomas sat on the loo and pondered with the wisdom of age.

After a while it seemed to him that there were sounds in the silence – they were faint and came from the direction of his house. He stood up and peered through the ventilation-hole – between the cracks in one of the shutters he saw a light, not the light of a lamp, but the wavering light that a candle might give. Then he thought he heard the sound of hammering and scraping and chipping. He thought of burglars – perhaps they had employed the boy as a scout, but why should burglars engage in what sounded more and more like a stealthy form of carpentry? Mr Thomas let out an experimental yell, but nobody answered. The noise could not even have reached his enemies.

# 4

Mike had gone home to bed, but the rest stayed. The question of leadership no longer concerned the gang. With nails, chisels, screwdrivers, anything that was sharp and penetrating, they moved around the inner walls worrying at the mortar between the bricks. They started too high, and it was Blackie who hit on the damp course and realized the work could be halved if they weakened the joints immediately above. It was a long, tiring, unamusing job, but at last it was finished. The gutted house stood there balanced on a few inches of mortar between the damp course and the bricks.

There remained the most dangerous task of all, out in the open at the edge of the bomb-site. Summers was sent to watch the road for passers-by, and Mr Thomas, sitting on the loo, heard clearly now the sound of sawing. It no longer came from the house, and that a little reassured him. He felt less concerned. Perhaps the other noises too had no significance.

A voice spoke to him through the hole. 'Mr Thomas.'

'Let me out,' Mr Thomas said sternly.

'Here's a blanket,' the voice said, and a long grey sausage was worked through the hole and fell in swathes over Mr Thomas's head.

'There's nothing personal,' the voice said. 'We want you to be comfortable tonight.'

'Tonight,' Mr Thomas repeated incredulously.

'Catch,' the voice said. 'Penny buns – we've buttered them, and sausage-rolls. We don't want you to starve, Mr Thomas.'

Mr Thomas pleaded desperately. 'A joke's a joke, boy. Let me out and I won't say a thing. I've got rheumatics. I got to sleep comfortable.'

'You wouldn't be comfortable, not in your house, you wouldn't. Not now.'

'What do you mean, boy?' But the footsteps receded. There was only the silence of night: no sound of sawing. Mr Thomas tried one more yell, but he was daunted and rebuked by the silence – a long way off an owl hooted and made away again on its muffled flight through the soundless world.

At seven next morning the driver came to fetch his lorry. He climbed into the seat and tried to start the engine. He was vaguely aware of a voice shouting, but it didn't concern him. At last the engine responded and he backed the lorry until it touched the great wooden shore that supported Mr Thomas's house. That way he could drive right out and down the street without reversing. The lorry moved forward, was momentarily checked as though something were pulling it from behind, and then went on to the sound of a long rumbling crash. The driver was astonished to see bricks bouncing ahead of him, while stones hit the roof of his cab. He put on his brakes. When he climbed out the whole landscape had suddenly altered. There was no house beside the car-park, only a hill of rubble. He went round and examined the back of his lorry for damage, and found a rope tied there that was still twisted at the other end round part of a wooden strut.

The driver again became aware of somebody shouting. It came from the wooden erection which was the nearest thing to a house in that desolation of broken brick. The driver climbed the smashed wall and unlocked the door. Mr Thomas came out of the loo. He was wearing a grey blanket to which flakes of pastry adhered. He gave a sobbing cry. 'My house,' he said. 'Where's my house?'

'Search me,' the driver said. His eye lit on the remains of a bath and what had once been a dresser and he began to laugh. There wasn't anything left anywhere.

'How dare you laugh,' Mr Thomas said. 'It was my house. My house.'

'I'm sorry,' the driver said, making heroic efforts, but when he remembered the sudden check of his lorry, the crash of bricks falling, he became convulsed again. One moment the house had stood there with such dignity between the bomb-sites like a man in a top hat, and then, bang, crash, there wasn't anything

left – not anything. He said, 'I'm sorry. I can't help it, Mr Thomas. There's nothing personal, but you got to admit it's funny.'
*1954*

# INTRODUCTION

'Ex Voto', Geraldine McCaughrean
'The War Prayer', Mark Twain

Mark Twain's 'The War Prayer' is a brilliant, scathing attack on militant patriotism. An old man interrupts a sermon in which the priest is praying for victory to add a prayer of his own and illuminate the inevitable consequences of one army's success.

Geraldine McCaughrean offers up a more sinister man of God – one whose black heart people have long ago seen right through. Both stories present characters who believe in their just wars. Both authors confront that belief and suggest that victory in war is meaningless.

Who do you think the authors believe to be the victims in war?

# EX VOTO

## Geraldine McCaughrean

As his sword hit the plaster, a spark flew, then the blade's tip snapped off. Hugh's breath escaped him in a heavy sob halfway to a laugh. That it should break now – this blade that had travelled so far with him! Having weathered the blazing desert heat, the freezing desert nights, having struck limbs from bodies, heads from shoulders, having driven chain-mail links into flesh like currants into dough, it chose now to snap, inside the chapel of this peaceful English monastery. Plaster fell on to his face, like quicklime on to a corpse.

Sir Hugh shrugged – well, would have shrugged but for the wound in his shoulder. The flesh had healed but not the joint beneath, which never would. He could already foresee the nicknames they would dub him: 'Lapwing', 'Hunchback', 'the Tilt' … What name would his mother call him, he wondered, if she proved still to be alive? He went back to gouging away at the wall of the nave. His bad shoulder ached. The pain no longer troubled Hugh; he had endured so much that it had lost the power even to annoy him.

Morning sunbeams, shining in over the rim of the high windows, also drove long blades of light into the plastered wall. Perhaps the sun too was carving its *ex-voto*, in thanks at having survived another night. How quiet it was, this place he had chanced upon. Unusually quiet, even for a monastery chapel.

'Devil toss you on his pitchfork, you thieving dog!' said a voice behind him and a blow across his back felled him to his knees. As he fell, he assessed the degree of pain, the likelihood of death. He also began counting seconds: he had learned precisely how long an enemy took to deliver a second blow. Before his attacker could hit him again, he had rolled over and up and lunged with his sword. If the tip had not been broken, it would have pierced the abbot's belly.

The abbot was holding the candle sconce like a quarter-staff, and his lips were drawn back off his teeth in a ferocious snarl.

'An *ex-voto*! I was carving an *ex-voto*!' cried Hugh in self-defence and the abbot, recognizing a cultured voice, stood the large candlestick back on its base.

'I thought you were prising the chains out of the wall,' he said (though he did not apologize). And now that Hugh looked, he could see that the beautiful wooden font had indeed been chained to the chapel wall. 'They pilfer. All the time, they pilfer, God rot them,' said the abbot. He examined the hole Hugh had made in the plaster. 'Poor effort.'

'Not for want of gratitude to my maker,' said Hugh. 'Only for want of a fit tool.'

The abbot promptly disappeared out of a side door and returned a minute later with a mason's awl that he tossed to the knight. 'I fine you one crown for scarring church fabric ... Here. You'll make a better job with this.' As Hugh paid, the abbot tried his hardest to see into the purse.

Hugh gladly laid aside his sword. It was much easier using the awl. He was able to scrape out the shape of a fluked cross around the dent he had already made. He worked on steadily, tongue creeping out of the corner of his mouth as he concentrated on his *ex-voto* – his note of thanks to God for bringing him safe home from the war.

He was not the first returning Crusader to carve on the chapel wall. Several 'fines' must have been paid to the abbot. Two dozen crosses were cut in the plaster – even into the marble floor around the font – some as deep as arrow slits, some as shallow as hastily dug graves. Hugh's heart filled with gratitude that these men, too, had survived the bloodbath of the Holy Wars – had dragged themselves home across desert, through hostile countries, escaped diseases, avoided capture or slavery or shipwreck or bandits or open wounds festering or rotten food … Each carved cross represented a miracle really.

His head also filled with the faces of those who had not survived – friends, comrades, yeomen of his own levy, his brother Luke …

'You use the devil's hand to work, I see,' said the abbot sourly.

'I took a hurt in my shoulder,' said Sir Hugh. 'I have to use my left hand.'

One question had rolled around inside Hugh all the way home, like a stone in his boot. Suddenly – he did not know why – it found its way out of his mouth. 'Why did God not grant us the victory, Father Abbot? I know, I know – serving the Lord is a privilege … But you would suppose – given that He called us to go on Crusade – that God would grant us the victory. Or why –'

The question gave the abbot no difficulty at all. 'Too many sinners among you,' he said. 'The feet of the army stumbled upon their own trespasses and they were mired in sin.' It sounded like a quotation from the Bible, though Sir Hugh could not place it. He tried to picture the great army of the Second Crusade, and behind it its siege engines, forges and field kitchens, and behind them – biggest of all – a vast bundle holding all the sins of the marching men, gradually dragging them to a standstill.

'But we went on the Crusade to be forgiven, Father! The priests told us it was our duty to go and our reward to be forgiven! One thousand years less in purgatory! Our accounts wiped clean! Our souls washed in the blood of the Heathen! Why did the victory go to the heathen, Father?'

'The ways of God are not our ways,' snapped the abbot glibly. 'You brought home other rewards, I dare swear. Loot? Plunder?'

Sir Hugh thought of the contents of his saddlebag. 'Something for my sweetheart,' he admitted.

The abbot shuddered with distaste at the mention of a sweetheart but still wanted to see what loot the knight had brought. So Hugh went outside to his horse, tethered in the monastery garden. He stayed to stroke her – the winded, galled, ringwormed nag that had once been the finest in the county. Hardship had made them the best of friends. He told her about the *ex-voto* he had carved and the horse nodded her head in approval. Then Hugh got the pomegranate out of his saddle-wallet and took it back into the chapel. He had picked it in the Holy Land. The hard rind was browner now, but still as hard as eggshell.

The abbot took hold of it with a look of disgust. 'Is this all?'

'We had to travel light. It was bad. At the end. Chaos. We were lucky to get away with our skins. The ones who did.' In the back of Hugh's head familiar monsters squirmed into view – the ones he tried so hard to block out: the pomegranate hanging on its tree; the men lying under that tree as though resting in its shade; its roots soaking up their blood. Perhaps the fruit of the pomegranate tree grew red from drinking the blood of the Crusades.

A cord ran down inside the abbot's skirts. He pulled out a bunch of keys and useful implements. With a knife he ringed the pomegranate and twisted it open. Some of the seeds fell out on to his foot. The juice stained his hands. Those hands will be sticky all day now, thought Hugh absently.

He did not trouble to grieve for the loss of the pomegranate. Such things are not important in comparison with being alive. And now that it was open, the fruit reminded him too much of things he had seen after a sword stroke cut through a helmet, a limb, a horse's flank.

'How many did you kill?' asked the abbot, sniffing the fruit dubiously and giving both halves back to Hugh.

'Sorry, Father?'

'How many heathens did you kill?'

Hugh shook his head. The colourful monsters

writhed in the back of his brain: black, blood-red, tripe-white, chestnut, sallow, bay … 'Fifty. Sixty, maybe.'

The abbot raised his hands, so that the sunlight fell on his fat white fingers. Hugh bent one knee, thinking to be blessed. But the abbot was simply doing his sums. 'Eight hundred crowns should void it,' he said.

'Father?'

'Well? Did you think to break the Sixth Commandment and not pay the price? *Thou shalt not kill*. The fine has been fixed at twelve crowns per head. Best pay me as much as you can here and now and receive forgiveness. You could wait until you reach your own estates, but the roads are rife with thieves, and if you were to die unshriven …'

Hunger and sickness had kept Hugh company all the way from Palestine. Now they gave him a push and he reeled with dizziness. 'I'm sorry. I fear I do not understand you, Father.'

The abbot pursed his lips impatiently. His face seemed to ask how such a stupid knight had managed to find his way home at all. 'Blood weighs heavy, young man. I counsel you earnestly to wash away your sins! Ransom your soul. Some piece of carving on a wall won't do.'

Hysteria, somewhere between laughter and tears, caught in Hugh's throat.

When the call to arms had come, his parents had dug deep to furnish him and his brother with horse, weaponry and armour, so that they might serve the holy cause – recapture Jerusalem for Christ and Christendom! Now Hugh alone was home again, penniless, his only wealth oozing from the broken rind of a pomegranate. And was his surcoat too soaked, his soul too sodden, his scabbard too brimful of blood for him to enter heaven?

'Let me be sure I understand you,' Hugh said slowly and deliberately. 'The Church sends us to war, telling us that fighting for Christ will save our souls. Then, when we come home, you tell us we are sinners for taking lives? And must buy back our innocence with twelve pieces of silver?' Rage flashed behind his eyes as red as blood.

What hatred had he ever felt for the dark-faced strangers who had confronted him over the rim of his shield, who had crossed swords with him, whose thighs had touched his as their horses collided? What wrong had he ever felt he was righting? How holy had it ever felt to wipe the sweat from his lip and taste blood on his glove?

Now this fat abbot, smug and supercilious, was telling him it had been for nothing – for less than nothing – had fitted him for nothing but damnation, had earned him nothing but the tortures of hell. And was his brother even now roasting in hell, for killing Moors at the Holy Church's command?

A red fog clouded Hugh's eyes. The same fog had helped him face a charging horde of Arab horsemen without turning tail, had let him torch a village and trample the dead under his horse's hoofs. Now it blinded him to the sacredness of his surroundings, the light-pierced beauty of the nave, the reverent respect owed to a minister of God. Hugh went for his sword. But of course he had laid it aside. His scabbard was empty.

All of a sudden, something flew through the sun-filled slit of the window above him and landed on the floor of the nave with a crack. It was a rock. Hugh stared at it, bewildered. More rocks hit the outside of the wall, with a noise like hoofs clipping flint. The abbot moved with remarkable speed to push shut the open door, shooting the bolt just as someone tried to enter.

Fuddled by hunger and fatigue, Hugh was slow to grasp what was going on. 'Are we under attack?'

The abbot was running full tilt from font to vestry to transept, bolting doors, shouting as he did so, 'Three thousand years in hell to you all! Devil gripe you, you godless Gadarene swine!'

As more rocks rattled down round and about him, Hugh recovered himself. The red fog cleared.

He slipped back into the role of Christian knight defending the True Faith. Who but the wicked would attack a monastery chapel? He only wished he could have brought his poor mare indoors.

Cakes of dung and half a rusty ploughshare came through the lancet windows. He retreated to the centre of the nave. Fists were beating on all the doors now, filling the nave with a clamour that reverberated through the choir stalls and up the yawning emptiness of the bell-tower. Birds and bats swooped in terror through the nave. Hugh's sword still lay by the font.

'Scum! Vermin! Devil slit you, you heathen plague rats!' bawled the abbot, his voice cracking like an old stirrup leather. 'By bell, book and candle I cut you off from all hope of heaven!' He ran to the vestry and fetched out a richly embroidered surplice.

At least the man means to die in the robes of his calling! thought Hugh. And he resolved to do his Christian duty as a knight and defend the abbot with his life's blood against whatever godless fiends were outside.

The fiends outside seemed to care nothing about damnation, but redoubled their efforts to break in. A tree branch hit the window and fell back on to the person who had thrown it, who cursed.

'Who *are* they?' Hugh asked. In his weary bewilderment he had begun to imagine Moorish faces, Moorish swords, Moorish pavilions massing outside this English monastery.

'The devil's brood, that's who!' panted the abbot, kneeling beside a gigantic coffer by the door, rattling a key in its lock. It was an intricate lock, its workings a maze of rods and junctions and curlicues filling the lid of the chest. But at last the mechanism grated and clanked, and the hasp was free. The abbot threw open the lid and began pulling out various leather bags, jute sacks and church plate. 'They'd sooner buy cheese and ale than pay their tithes to me!' His spittle spattered the plates and chalices as he wrapped them in the embroidered surplice. As he worked, he shouted at the top of his voice: 'Sons of Gomorrah! Worshippers of Mammon!'

(Daughters of Gomorrah too, to judge by the shrill taunts coming through the lepers' window.) Who could they be, these witches and demons who felt no fear of God or His ministers?

'Thankless serpents and vipers!' hissed the abbot, knotting together the corners of the surplice and dragging it to the side door. 'You must hold them off, knight, while I ... while I ... save the treasures of St Ivo!' Suddenly remembering the saintly relic kept under the altar in a lead-lined casket, he dragged it out and shunted it down the choir, like a child trying to toboggan on thin snow. 'Want to kiss it?' he grunted.

Sir Hugh knelt and kissed the casket as it skidded past him, its hasp catching him a blow across the nose. The heart of St Ivo encased in lead made a screaming noise as the nails in its base scraped the marble floor.

'Why does no one come to our aid?' Hugh asked, realizing, for the first time, that he had seen no monks other than the abbot since riding up to the chapel door an hour before.

'Gone already – like rats from a leaky ship. Judgement fall on them! Fire and brimstone scorch their dirty hides!'

Hugh had the nightmarish impression that he must have brought war home with him, along with the lice in his hair, the fleas in his blanket, the ringworm in his horse. It was as if the ghostly spectre of war had ridden home behind him, sharing his saddle, resting its sharp chin on his shoulder. Now chaos would engulf the rolling green English countryside – and it would all be his fault!

'In the name of Christ, I charge you to defend this place!' commanded the abbot, thrusting Hugh's sword at him so that he dropped the pomegranate. 'I must save the relic of St Ivo! Defend this place, knight, and God will reward you!' And, dragging the heavy casket across the brass effigies in the aisle, the abbot disappeared into the shadowy transept.

And Hugh did wait, sword in hand.

A lifetime of obedience to the commands of Mother Church is not easily dislodged. Since childhood, the words 'Church' and 'Goodness' had been tangled tight in his breast: he was far too weary to wrench them apart now. Stones rattled down around him, and smoke began to crawl in under the doors. From time to time some kind of battering ram jarred the lock. Glancing down, Hugh saw that St Ivo's heart had crushed one half of the pomegranate and smeared it like blood and gristle across the brass faces of the dead.

The booming of the battering ram shook all logic out of his head. Once they broke in, how long could he last before they killed him? And even if he could kill every last one of them, how many more years would he have to suffer for it in purgatory before the sin was flayed from his soul?

He began to see demons clambering down the bell-ropes hand over hand, leering, jeering and cackling: *Got you! Tricked you! Fooled you! Caught you! Thou shalt not kill! Thou shalt not kill! We'll take you where we took your brother! Thou shalt not escape us now!* Hugh stood stock still, muscles so rigid, breath so pent, that he felt he was turning to stone like the effigies who lay along their tombs staring up into the vaulted roof. At last, with a splintering of wood, the door lurched open ...

***

After a moment, a flock of farm boys, reddlemen, shepherds, quarrymen, housewives, weavers, hedgers and children nosed their way nervously into the church. Not Moors, then, not savage, murderous heathens, thirsty for blood. Locals. The coloured light of the chapel washed over their faces and softened their scowls.

''Ems gone at last, then, them fat leeches?' called a tinsmith to the knight standing halfway up the aisle.

'Good riddance,' said a widow, devoutly crossing herself and curtseying to the altar. 'Helping themselves to anything they fancied. Breaking their vows. Dipping their hands in our pockets. Fleecing us these twenty years! Got no more conscience than dead ferrets, them beggars.'

They gathered glumly around the empty coffer until someone dragged it away as loot. The widow took the altar cloth, folding it four times and placing it on her head. There was little else left; the deserting monks had taken all they could carry.

Hugh watched them as he might people in a dream. He saw a miller step on the other half of the pomegranate and bend to study the mess, flummoxed by the oddness of what he had trodden in.

'Leeches, bleeding us white they were,' remarked a weaver, eyeing the knight's sword nervously as it twitched in his grasp. 'Had a bad harvest last year, but did they care 'bout our sorrows? Did they ask less? Did they tighten their belts? Not them! The religious life, they called it. We called it living off our backs. What's a monk anyway, but a man with a shaved head? Look at me.' And he showed the crown of his head where baldness had given him the look of a monk without the greedy, grasping nature of one. 'Do that give me the right to help myself to a slice of my neighbour's dinner?'

The widow came and peered at Hugh, her eyes straying over his features, and she absently licked a fingerful of apron and began to clean his face for him. 'Blessings on the Virgin Mary for bringing you safe home to your mother – whoever you are. I lost my men at Damascus. If you knows where in God's earth that is, you knows more than I do. These monks – they thinks up wars to take our husbands and sons from us, but they stays home themselves, living off the widows' sweat and toil!'

'No! Surely it was God above who ...' began Hugh but had to stop; the woman was busy folding back his lips to polish his teeth.

'Do not you believe it, lad! War's always the idea of men! God's just the excuse. Afterwards, men keeps the loot. All God gets is the blame.'

'Might be different, other places,' said the

reddleman, pursuing his own train of thought. 'Monks might be saints, some of 'em, for all I know. But here … We've had all of them we can stomach. Been like our own private war 'twixt them and us these two months past,' he explained to the knight. 'A nest of wasps is less of a curse than a nest of godless monks.'

A ploughboy armed with a mattock took a swing at the chain securing the font to the wall. He dislodged a cloud of plaster, and cracks spread out from the hole, crazing the *ex-votos* of a dozen Crusaders.

Then a stir of excitement fetched everyone to the side door of the chapel to see a thing of interest. The boy with the mattock prised open the casket and laid bare the heart of St Ivo. It had never meant as much to the abbot as saving his hide.

And to do that, he had helped himself to Hugh's mare and made good his escape.

# THE WAR PRAYER

## Mark Twain

It was a time of great and exalting excitement. The country was up in arms, the war was on, in every breast burned the holy fire of patriotism; the drums were beating, the bands playing, the toy pistols popping, the bunched firecrackers hissing and spluttering; on every hand and far down the receding and fading spread of roofs and balconies a fluttering wilderness of flags flashed in the sun; daily the young volunteers marched down the wide avenue gay and fine in their new uniforms, the proud fathers and mothers and sisters and sweethearts cheering them with voices choked with happy emotion as they swung by; nightly the packed mass meetings listened, panting, to patriot oratory which stirred the deepest deeps of their hearts, and which they interrupted at briefest intervals with cyclones of applause, the tears running down their cheeks the while; in the churches the pastors preached devotion to flag and country, and invoked the

God of Battles beseeching His aid in our good cause in outpourings of fervid eloquence which moved every listener. It was indeed a glad and gracious time, and the half dozen rash spirits that ventured to disapprove of the war and cast a doubt upon its righteousness straightway got such a stern and angry warning that for their personal safety's sake they quickly shrank out of sight and offended no more in that way.

Sunday morning came – next day the battalions would leave for the front; the church was filled; the volunteers were there, their young faces alight with martial dreams – visions of the stern advance, the gathering momentum, the rushing charge, the flashing sabres, the flight of the foe, the tumult, the enveloping smoke, the fierce pursuit, the surrender! Then home from the war, bronzed heroes, welcomed, adored, submerged in golden seas of glory! With the volunteers sat their dear ones, proud, happy, and envied by the neighbours and friends who had no sons and brothers to send forth to the field of honour, there to win for the flag, or, failing, die the noblest of noble deaths. The service proceeded; a war chapter from the Old Testament was read; the first prayer was said; it was followed by an organ burst that shook the building, and with one impulse the house rose, with glowing eyes and beating hearts, and poured out that tremendous invocation:

'God the all-terrible! Thou who ordainest! Thunder thy clarion and lightning thy sword!'

Then came the 'long' prayer. None could remember the like of it for passionate pleading and moving and beautiful language. The burden of its supplication was, that an ever-merciful and benignant Father of us all would watch over our noble young soldiers, and aid, comfort, and encourage them in their patriotic work; bless them, shield them in the day of battle and the hour of peril, bear them in His mighty hand, make them strong and confident, invincible in the bloody onset; help them to crush the foe, grant to them and to their flag and country imperishable honour and glory –

An aged stranger entered and moved with slow and noiseless step up the main aisle, his eyes fixed upon the minister, his long body clothed in a robe that reached to his feet, his head bare, his white hair descending in a frothy cataract to his shoulders, his seamy face unnaturally pale, pale even to ghastliness. With all eyes following him and wondering, he made his silent way; without pausing, he ascended to the preacher's side and stood there waiting. With shut lids the preacher, unconscious of his presence, continued with his moving prayer, and at last finished it with the words, uttered in fervent appeal, 'Bless our arms, grant us the victory, O Lord our God, Father and Protector of our land and flag!'

The stranger touched his arm, motioned him to step aside – which the startled minister did – and took his place. During some moments he surveyed the spellbound audience with solemn eyes, in which burned an uncanny light; then in a deep voice he said:

'I come from the Throne – bearing a message from Almighty God!' The words smote the house with a shock; if the stranger perceived it he gave no attention. 'He has heard the prayer of His servant your shepherd, and will grant it if such shall be your desire after I, His messenger, shall have explained to you its import – that is to say, its full import. For it is like unto many of the prayers of men, in that it asks for more than he who utters it is aware of – except he pause and think.

'God's servant and yours has prayed his prayer. Has he paused and taken thought? Is it one prayer? No, it is two – one uttered, the other not. Both have reached the ear of Him Who heareth all supplications, the spoken and the unspoken. Ponder this – keep it in mind. If you would beseech a blessing upon yourself, beware! lest without intent you invoke a curse upon a neighbour at the same time. If you pray for the blessing of rain upon your crop which needs it, by that act you are possibly praying for a curse upon some neighbour's crop which may not need rain and can be injured by it.

'You have heard your servant's prayer – the uttered part of it. I am commissioned of God to put into words the other part of it – that part which the pastor – and also you in your hearts – fervently prayed silently. And ignorantly and unthinkingly? God grant that it was so! You heard these words: "Grant us the victory, O Lord our God!" That is sufficient. The whole of the uttered prayer is compact into those pregnant words. Elaborations were not necessary. When you have prayed for victory you have prayed for many unmentioned results which follow victory – must follow it, cannot help but follow it. Upon the listening spirit of God fell also the unspoken part of the prayer. He commandeth me to put it into words. Listen!

'O Lord our Father, our young patriots, idols of our hearts, go forth to battle – be Thou near them! With them – in spirit – we also go forth from the sweet peace of our beloved firesides to smite the foe. O Lord our God, help us to tear their soldiers to bloody shreds with our shells; help us to cover their smiling fields with the pale forms of their patriot dead; help us to drown the thunder of the guns with the shrieks of their wounded, writhing in pain; help us to lay waste their humble homes with a hurricane of fire; help us to wring the hearts of their unoffending widows with unavailing grief; help us to turn them out roofless with little children to wander unfriended the wastes of their desolated land in rags and hunger and thirst, sports of the sun flames of summer and the icy winds of winter, broken in spirit, worn with travail, imploring Thee for the refuge of the grave and denied it – for our sakes who adore Thee, Lord, blast their hopes, blight their lives, protract their bitter pilgrimage, make heavy their steps, water their way with their tears, stain the white snow with the blood of their wounded feet! We ask it, in the spirit of love, of Him Who is the Source of Love, and Who is the ever-faithful refuge and friend of all that are sore beset and seek His aid with humble and contrite hearts. Amen.'

(After a pause)

'Ye have prayed it; if ye still desire it, speak! The messenger of the Most High waits!'

It was believed afterward that the man was a lunatic, because there was no sense in what he said.

# INTRODUCTION

'The Princess Spy', Jamila Gavin
'His Last Bow', Arthur Conan Doyle

Few functions in war are quite so mysterious, so instinctively exciting, as that of the spy. On secret missions, undercover, behind enemy lines, they fight wars all on their own.

Sherlock Holmes is brought out of retirement in 'His Last Bow' to conduct a mission for the British during the First World War. Being Sherlock Holmes, of course, he is in possession of an instinct for brilliant disguises and a superhuman brain – the perfect spy!

Jamila Gavin's story about an eager young British agent captured by the Nazis in Paris is more brutal. Noor is not superhuman. She is mistrusted by her superiors, abandoned by her colleagues and tortured by her captors.

It would be interesting to consider the following two questions applied to each story:

Who is the spy ultimately loyal to?
In what way does the spy defeat the enemy?

# THE PRINCESS SPY

## Code Name: Madeleine

## Jamila Gavin

*Others think they know me
But I am mine; what I am, I am.*

In the darkness I see no light. But there is a light in my soul which shines out and illumines my prison cell.

*What can the tiger catch in the dark corners of his own lair?*

In the darkness I hear no sound, but in my head I hear music, of course! Music.

*Only sweet-voiced birds are imprisoned.*

In my mouth I would taste only bitterness if I didn't have the memory of sweet almonds and lover's kisses.

They keep me chained to the wall like a savage dog, but I am a swallow, soaring, circling high on the air currents. Whatever they do to me, I will not let myself down. I have not betrayed my country, I have not betrayed my masters. I am a princess. The blood of the great Rajah, Tipoo Sultan, runs in my veins. I am of the warrior class. They can interrogate me all they want and torture me too, but I will not betray myself.

Her name was Noor.

Her father was an Indian prince, Hazrat Inayat Khan, a Muslim, a musician and a Sufi mystic. His reputation spread far and wide for his wise counselling – even as far as Moscow. There, the strange, powerful Russian Orthodox mystic monk, Rasputin, asked him to come to the Kremlin palace and bring his Sufi philosophy of peace and love to comfort the Tsar of All Russias, Tsar Nicholas, in his time of trouble. Russia was in turmoil. Nicholas didn't understand why. How could he, closed away in his palaces, as far removed from his people as the sun is from the earth?

So, along with his young American wife, Nora, Hazrat arrived in Moscow. Their first child, Noor, was born in the Kremlin palace on 2 January 1914; when Europe was bristling with quarrels, intrigues and assassinations, leading up to the outbreak of the First World War that August. Russia, too, was seething with unrest and things were leading inexorably towards revolution.

The stone walls surround me, yet the chains fall from my limbs and I am an infant again, crawling up the long scarlet-carpeted staircase in the Russian palace. There is an outburst of girlish laughter, and a flurry of princesses surround me like swans, gathering me up, pinching my cheeks and passing me round like a parcel: Olga, Tatiana, Maria and Anastasia. 'Let me hold her! Let me!' Their voices tinkle like bells.

'Darling Alexis!' The princesses draw in their little brother – their precious boy who, one day, will be Tsar of All Russias. 'Here. Careful now, don't drop her!' and I am passed into the arms of a boy who looks at me with sad, solemn eyes.

Their eyes gleam at me through the years of darkness. 'They came for us,' they seem to say. 'Now they have come for you.'

Look! There I am again, bundled up in furs, crammed in among the Russian princesses on the back of a sleigh, pulled by jingling horses, flying across the flat, white, rigid landscape, and plunging into birch forests, their branches drooping with snow. 'Baba Yaga, the witch, is after us,' they whispered in my ear, making me shriek with joyful terror.

They are all dead now. The tsar and his queen, my lovely swan princesses, all captured – not by Baba Yaga, but by the Bolshevik revolutionaries, who shot them all those years ago; Alexis too – my little tsaravitch.

My father's face bends over me so tenderly. His

beard is like a cloud and his dark eyes are deep pools of mystery. 'Go to sleep, my little hare,' he murmurs.

A hare? Am I the hare? Lord Buddha came as a hare, and was willing to allow himself to be eaten to feed a hungry person.

'Tell me another story,' she whimpers in the dark.

How she loved stories and made them tell her more, more, and when there were no more to tell, Noor made up her own.

Princess Noor was born to enchant. She was beautiful and talented. A child of the Muses – full of poetry, stories, dance and music. A child of rhythm – but a rhythm of her own – shy, soaring, circling among the ideas and philosophies that her father taught her.

How could her stiff English masters understand that?

When she stood before them – this dark, gleaming young woman who looked more suited to the bohemian cafes of Paris than the tight-lipped, English-public-school discipline of the War Office – they must have asked themselves, 'What on earth has she to offer?'

'Like the hare, my little princess, you can offer yourself.' My father's voice counselled me in my head.

Oh, why did you have to die, dear father?

He is the only one I weep for. My torturers have made me scream and cry as they have tried in vain to make me talk, but those tears are different; they are because of my physical pain. The pain which makes me truly weep is deeper; it is the pain of betrayal and because I no longer know who is my friend and who my enemy. It is the pain of loss because you are dead and gone. Oh, Papa! We were all thrown into such agony when we heard of your death in India while we were so far away from you in Paris. Mama locked herself away in her room and would not come out. We couldn't bear to think that never again would we hear your music, never again hear your deep, silken voice and listen to your wise words. Yet now, in this empty silence, you speak to me. You are here after all, to give me courage.

'Death is just stepping into the light, dear daughter. Remember the hare? As he entered the fire to give his body so that others could eat, the fairy of light came and made the flames as cool as water.'

*We are waves whose stillness is non-being.*

It was 1940. The Nazis had overrun almost the whole of Europe and were now at the gates of Paris. 'We have to leave immediately,' Noor begged her mother, who had shunned the world for twelve years, leaving Noor to be the responsible one. 'We must get out now.' With great difficulty, she persuaded her mother to flee. They all joined a long train of refugees and headed for the coast, and managed to get on to the last boat leaving for England. There, Noor and her brother wanted to help the war effort. He joined the Royal Air Force and she the Women's Auxiliary Air Force – the WAAF – and was assigned to its transport section. She was keen and dedicated. But surely she could do more?

Pinstripe-suited men discussed her, sitting on one side of a long, polished table. 'She asks to do more? We need more people in Paris. We could use her, perhaps.'

They summoned her before them.

Here in the darkness, Paris gleams out in my mind. Beautiful Paris. The boulevards are scattered with sunlight. I walk gaily, composing tunes in my head on my way to school, sniffing the honey-roasted peanuts they sell in the Luxembourg Gardens, as I cut through to St-Germain-des-Prés. I wriggle my fingers, remembering the exercises I have been practising. Paris is my home; it's where my friends are. It's where I feel alive and truly myself.

'If you send me to France, you are sending me home,' I told them.

***

'Let's see,' said Pinstripe, looking at the notes and files in front of him. 'You have been living in Paris with your mother, brother and sisters for the last seventeen years. Music student, writer of stories –' he glanced down at his notes – 'for children? You've broadcast on Paris radio – so your French is fluent – and you know the city well.'

'It's my home,' she repeated. 'I want to help.'

'Yes, well …' They conferred while she waited outside. 'Perhaps she would be of use,' said one.

'It will be dangerous,' said another with some compassion. 'If they catch her, she'll be shot.'

'It's war. Sacrifices have to be made.'

To the men of the War Office she looked so unsuited to this work – too otherworldly, too innocent, too much of a butterfly. Not British. Most were sceptical. After all, they had never sent in a woman radio operative before. What's more, she was an Indian. India was already in conflict with the British – trying to kick them out of India. Could they be sure that she could be trusted?

'If she can't be trusted,' a cold, dark voice spoke, 'all the better for playing a game with, my dear.'

The game. What game? Everyone knew there was a game, but so few knew who the players were and what the rules of the game were.

'Send her into France as one of our operatives. Give her a radio. Ask her to send and receive messages. We'll send her information – false information. She's sure to be caught and sure to be interrogated. At first, she won't speak, but – I know these sorts of people – she'll crack. She'll spill the beans. But they'll be our beans, and they'll swallow them whole.'

So she received her instructions. 'We want you to go to France. Meet up with the Resistance; be a radio operative. You will be given a transmitter and will learn the radio game,' they told her.

She was registered in her mother's name – Norah Baker – and her training began. For long weeks, she learned how to operate the radio, how to use the codes and ciphers they would give her. They told her about the Resistance cells all over France, full of people working to free France and the rest of Europe from the Nazis.

She would have to be flown in at night, landing in a field. She would have to connect with other agents and sympathizers, and be part of a group. She must learn how to collect information and radio it back to them, to live a double life. Her cover name was to be Jeanne-Marie Regnier, her code name, 'Madeleine'.

I am flying, flying! How beautiful. The darkness of my cell is illumined by the moon. I felt close to heaven, then, as we flew; and close to you, Papa, with the stars all around and the sea glistening below. How small I felt too. Infinitesimal. How could I make any difference?

*Yes, daughter, you are but a drop of water in an illimitable sea, but each drop is there to make up the consciousness of the whole ocean.*

The world looked marvellously tranquil in the cloudy moonshine that June night, when the Lysander took off from England. So peaceful. Impossible to think of the terrors and dangers that awaited her.

Suddenly, from far below, a shower of sparks from a fire sprayed upwards into the air like fireflies. 'That's them!' muttered the pilot, and the little plane circled and dropped lower and lower. It hadn't seemed real till then. Just one of her stories in which she was a character – a heroine: brave, unafraid, ready to die for the good of the world. Suddenly, she felt terror.

Here in my dark silent cell, my heart is thumping. I am afraid again. They will come for me soon.

The wheels struck the ground. There was a fierce bumping as the Lysander hurtled over the rough field. The dark shadows of trees whipped by like a smear from a paintbrush. Would they ever stop? They stopped, but the propellers kept spinning. The engine noise sounded dangerously loud.

'Out, out!' they yelled, pushing Noor through the door.

She was already dressed to look like a nursemaid. She was to pretend to be on her way to Paris to look after an old lady. So she was wearing a war-worn but well-tailored suit, a beret over her black short hair and black walking shoes. She would look as if she was on her way back from leave. They tossed her suitcase out to her; shabby and scratched, but hidden within its false lining, under her nurse's apron and cap, were her transmitter and her instructions.

'You will meet Garry,' they had told her. 'Your network is called Prospero. He will take you to them.'

No sooner had she leaped to the ground than the Lysander was already moving again and was skyborne – before she'd even turned to meet the man standing in the shadows.

He grasped her hand in the darkness. '*Viens. Vite!*' He snatched her suitcase with his other hand and began to run, tugging her along. They must get away from the field. Someone may have heard the plane. The Germans could be on their way. Already Noor had a stitch in her side; she was bent double, gasping – but kept running, allowing him to drag her along, pushing her through hedges and over stiles. At last they reached a small clearing. A car was waiting. Someone opened the door. 'Get in.' The case was thrown into the boot, then they were off – driving without lights – and hit the road to Paris.

'Garry!' My heart is thumping again. I call out his name. It has a hollow ring in this dark stone cell. 'Where are you now?'

Where are any of them? Gilbert, Antoine, Marguerite, Valentin. Some are dead. She had only been in Paris a week when the Nazis rounded up nearly all of the cell called Prospero. There was treachery everywhere, but the Gestapo didn't know her yet, so she slipped away and kept up radio contact with London.

She moved from one dreary apartment to another, hanging her aerial out of the windows to pick up signals from London, while trying to evade the direction-finding trucks which roamed the streets listening out for illegal transmissions.

I can still laugh – a croaking, gulping, last-gasp laugh – when I remember one fool of a Nazi coming in on me as I tried to fix up my aerial. He thought it was a washing line and helped me.

***

She lived like this for three months, the only British radio operative in Paris still free, still transmitting to London – staying on air a few minutes at a time, then moving on. A man called 'B' arrived from England to check out what was left of the Resistance.

'Come home with me,' he advised. 'You know you'll be shot if they catch you?'

She refused. 'They don't know me. I can still go on working for you. There's no one else left. You need me.' So 'B' returned without her.

But the Nazis were after her. Somehow they got to know her code name – Madeleine. Someone had betrayed her. She arrived back to her apartment one day to find a Gestapo officer in her room.

'She was like a wild cat,' he had reported later. She fought and bit and tried to get out. 'I had to pull a gun on her.' He phoned for help and other officers arrived. They ransacked her room and found her transmitter, notebooks, codes and ciphers. They took her to their headquarters at the Avenue Foch for interrogation.

'Just tell us all you know. Give us names, contacts. Tell us what the British are planning to do.'

'My name is Norah Baker. My number is 9901 – assistant section officer for the Women's Auxiliary Air Force Transport Service,' was all she would tell them.

'You're a fool.' They shook their heads with false

pity. 'You'll soon speak. Take her away.'

She made another desperate attempt to escape by climbing through a window and slithering across the rooftops. But they caught her and dragged her back.

She was now classified as a 'dangerous prisoner'.

They hurt me, Papa. They hurt me so much.

'We already know everything,' sneered the Gestapo. 'Your colleague broke. We know all about the plans. You might as well give in and save yourself more pain.'

'My name is Norah Baker, number 9901 …' She refused to give more than her name, rank and number.

Her masters thought she would break in the end. It was part of the plan. She would pass on false information; would tell them there was a plan to invade, that the Allies would land in Calais – not Normandy. But after five weeks of fierce interrogation, she stayed silent.

*Love is action; action is knowledge; knowledge is truth; truth is love.*

She was put on a train to Karlsruhe in Germany. There she stayed for ten months, in solitary confinement, shackled in chains. In September 1944 she was put on another train.

So this is where I am, Papa; Dachau. Not many people walk out alive from here. There are three other women from my section. We will meet for the first time in a few moments. I can hear the first birdsong of dawn. Yes – even in my cell, their song reaches me. I hear footsteps. They are coming.

*'Awake! For morning in the bowl of night has flung the stone that put the stars to flight.'*

Four women were taken out at dawn to a place all strewn with sand.

The sand is stained with blood.
I am a hare.

They were told to kneel. Four women – strangers to each other till then – held hands like sisters and knelt down together. An SS man came up behind them and, one by one, shot them dead.

Postscript: Princess Noor Inayat Khan was posthumously awarded the George Cross by the British and the Croix de Guerre by the French.

# HIS LAST BOW

## An Epilogue of Sherlock Holmes

# Arthur Conan Doyle

It was nine o'clock at night upon the second of August – the most terrible August in the history of the world. One might have thought already that God's curse hung heavy over a degenerate world, for there was an awesome hush and a feeling of vague expectancy in the sultry and stagnant air. The sun had long set, but one blood-red gash like an open wound lay low in the distant west. Above, the stars were shining brightly, and below, the lights of the shipping glimmered in the bay. The two famous Germans stood beside the stone parapet of the garden walk, with the long, low, heavily gabled house behind them, and they looked down upon the broad sweep of the beach at the foot of the great chalk cliff in which Von Bork, like some wandering eagle, had perched himself four years before. They stood with their heads close together, talking in low, confidential tones. From below the two glowing ends of their cigars might have been the smouldering eyes of some malignant fiend looking down in the darkness.

A remarkable man this Von Bork – a man who could hardly be matched among all the devoted agents of the Kaiser. It was his talents which had first recommended him for the English mission, the most important mission of all, but since he had taken it over those talents had become more and more manifest to the half-dozen people in the world who were really in touch with the truth. One of these was his present companion, Baron Von Herling, the chief secretary of the legation, whose huge 100-horse-power Benz car was blocking the country lane as it waited to waft its owner back to London.

'So far as I can judge the trend of events, you will probably be back in Berlin within the week,' the secretary was saying. 'When you get there, my dear Von Bork, I think you will be surprised at the welcome you will receive. I happen to know what is thought in the highest quarters of your work in this country.' He was a huge man, the secretary, deep, broad and tall, with a slow, heavy fashion of speech which had been his main asset in his political career.

Von Bork laughed.

'They are not very hard to deceive,' he remarked. 'A more docile, simple folk could not be imagined.'

'I don't know about that,' said the other

thoughtfully. 'They have strange limits and one must learn to observe them. It is that surface simplicity of theirs which makes a trap for the stranger. One's first impression is that they are entirely soft. Then one comes suddenly upon something very hard, and you know that you have reached the limit and must adapt yourself to the fact. They have, for example, their insular conventions which simply MUST be observed.'

'Meaning "good form" and that sort of thing?' Von Bork sighed as one who had suffered much.

'Meaning British prejudice in all its queer manifestations. As an example I may quote one of my own worst blunders – I can afford to talk of my blunders, for you know my work well enough to be aware of my successes. It was on my first arrival. I was invited to a weekend gathering at the country house of a cabinet minister. The conversation was amazingly indiscreet.'

Von Bork nodded. 'I've been there,' said he dryly.

'Exactly. Well, I naturally sent a resumé of the information to Berlin. Unfortunately our good chancellor is a little heavy-handed in these matters, and he transmitted a remark which showed that he was aware of what had been said. This, of course, took the trail straight up to me. You've no idea the harm that it did me. There was nothing soft about our

British hosts on that occasion, I can assure you. I was two years living it down. Now you, with this sporting pose of yours – '

'No, no, don't call it a pose. A pose is an artificial thing. This is quite natural. I am a born sportsman. I enjoy it.'

'Well, that makes it the more effective. You yacht against them, you hunt with them, you play polo, you match them in every game, your four-in-hand takes the prize at Olympia. I have even heard that you go the length of boxing with the young officers. What is the result? Nobody takes you seriously. You are a "good old sport", "quite a decent fellow for a German", a hard-drinking, night-club, knock-about-town, devil-may-care young fellow. And all the time this quiet country house of yours is the centre of half the mischief in England, and the sporting squire the most astute secret-service man in Europe. Genius, my dear Von Bork – genius!'

'You flatter me, Baron. But certainly I may claim my four years in this country have not been unproductive. I've never shown you my little store. Would you mind stepping in for a moment?'

The door of the study opened straight on to the terrace. Von Bork pushed it back, and, leading the way, he clicked the switch of the electric light. He then closed the door behind the bulky form which followed him and carefully adjusted the heavy curtain over the latticed window. Only when all these precautions had been taken and tested did he turn his sunburned aquiline face to his guest.

'Some of my papers have gone,' said he. 'When my wife and the household left yesterday for Flushing they took the less important with them. I must, of course, claim the protection of the embassy for the others.'

'Your name has already been filed as one of the personal suite. There will be no difficulties for you or your baggage. Of course, it is just possible that we may not have to go. England may leave France to her fate. We are sure that there is no binding treaty between them.'

'And Belgium?'

'Yes, and Belgium, too.'

Von Bork shook his head. 'I don't see how that could be. There is a definite treaty there. She could never recover from such a humiliation.'

'She would at least have peace for the moment.'

'But her honour?'

'Tut, my dear sir, we live in a utilitarian age. Honour is a medieval conception. Besides England is not ready. It is an inconceivable thing, but even our special war tax of fifty million, which one would think made our purpose as clear as if we had advertised it on the front page of the Times, has not roused these people from their slumbers. Here and there one hears a question. It is my business to find an answer. Here and there also there is an irritation. It is my business to soothe it. But I can assure you that so far as the essentials go – the storage of munitions, the preparation for submarine attack, the arrangements for making high explosives – nothing is prepared. How, then, can England come in, especially when we have stirred her up such a devil's brew of Irish civil war, window-breaking Furies, and God knows what to keep her thoughts at home.'

'She must think of her future.'

'Ah, that is another matter. I fancy that in the future we have our own very definite plans about England, and that your information will be very vital to us. It is today or tomorrow with Mr. John Bull. If he prefers today we are perfectly ready. If it is tomorrow we shall be more ready still. I should think they would be wiser to fight with allies than without them, but that is their own affair. This week is their week of destiny. But you were speaking of your papers.' He sat in the armchair with the light shining upon his broad bald head, while he puffed sedately at his cigar.

The large oak-panelled, book-lined room had a curtain hung in the further corner. When this was drawn it disclosed a large, brass-bound safe. Von

Bork detached a small key from his watch chain, and after some considerable manipulation of the lock he swung open the heavy door.

'Look!' said he, standing clear, with a wave of his hand.

The light shone vividly into the opened safe, and the secretary of the embassy gazed with an absorbed interest at the rows of stuffed pigeon-holes with which it was furnished. Each pigeon-hole had its label, and his eyes as he glanced along them read a long series of such titles as 'Fords', 'Harbour-defences', 'Aeroplanes', 'Ireland', 'Egypt', 'Portsmouth forts', 'The Channel', 'Rosythe' and a score of others. Each compartment was bristling with papers and plans.

'Colossal!' said the secretary. Putting down his cigar he softly clapped his fat hands.

'And all in four years, Baron. Not such a bad show for the hard-drinking, hard-riding country squire. But the gem of my collection is coming and there is the setting all ready for it.' He pointed to a space over which 'Naval Signals' was printed.

'But you have a good dossier there already.'

'Out of date and waste paper. The Admiralty in some way got the alarm and every code has been changed. It was a blow, Baron – the worst setback in my whole campaign. But thanks to my cheque-book and the good Altamont all will be well tonight.'

The Baron looked at his watch and gave a guttural exclamation of disappointment.

'Well, I really can wait no longer. You can imagine that things are moving at present in Carlton Terrace and that we have all to be at our posts. I had hoped to be able to bring news of your great coup. Did Altamont name no hour?'

Von Bork pushed over a telegram.

> Will come without fail to-night and bring new sparking plugs. Altamont.

'Sparking plugs, eh?'

'You see he poses as a motor expert and I keep a full garage. In our code everything likely to come up is named after some spare part. If he talks of a radiator it is a battleship, of an oil pump a cruiser, and so on. Sparking plugs are naval signals.'

'From Portsmouth at midday,' said the secretary, examining the superscription. 'By the way, what do you give him?'

'Five hundred pounds for this particular job. Of course he has a salary as well.'

'The greedy rogue. They are useful, these traitors, but I grudge them their blood money.'

'I grudge Altamont nothing. He is a wonderful worker. If I pay him well, at least he delivers the goods, to use his own phrase. Besides he is not a traitor. I assure you that our most pan-Germanic Junker is a sucking dove in his feelings towards England as compared with a real bitter Irish-American.'

'Oh, an Irish-American?'

'If you heard him talk you would not doubt it. Sometimes I assure you I can hardly understand him. He seems to have declared war on the King's English as well as on the English king. Must you really go? He may be here any moment.'

'No. I'm sorry, but I have already overstayed my time. We shall expect you early tomorrow, and when you get that signal book through the little door on the Duke of York's steps you can put a triumphant Finis to your record in England. What! Tokay!' He indicated a heavily sealed dust-covered bottle which stood with two high glasses upon a salver.

'May I offer you a glass before your journey?'

'No, thanks. But it looks like revelry.'

'Altamont has a nice taste in wines, and he took a fancy to my Tokay. He is a touchy fellow and needs humouring in small things. I have to study him, I assure you.' They had strolled out on to the terrace again, and along it to the further end where at a touch from the Baron's chauffeur the great car shivered and chuckled. 'Those are the lights of Harwich, I suppose,' said the secretary, pulling on his dust coat. 'How still and peaceful it all seems. There may be other lights within the week, and the English coast a less tranquil place! The heavens, too, may not be quite so peaceful if all that the good Zeppelin promises us comes true. By the way, who is that?'

Only one window showed a light behind them; in it there stood a lamp, and beside it, seated at a table, was a dear old ruddy-faced woman in a country cap. She was bending over her knitting and stopping occasionally to stroke a large black cat upon a stool beside her.

'That is Martha, the only servant I have left.'

The secretary chuckled.

'She might almost personify Britannia,' said he, 'with her complete self-absorption and general air of comfortable somnolence. Well, au revoir, Von Bork!' With a final wave of his hand he sprang into the car, and a moment later the two golden cones from the headlights shot through the darkness. The secretary lay back in the cushions of the luxurious limousine, with his thoughts so full of the impending European tragedy that he hardly observed that as his car swung round the village street it nearly passed over a little Ford coming in the opposite direction.

Von Bork walked slowly back to the study when the last gleams of the motor lamps had faded into the distance. As he passed he observed that his old housekeeper had put out her lamp and retired. It was a new experience to him, the silence and darkness of his widespread house, for his family and household had been a large one. It was a relief to him, however, to think that they were all in safety and that, but for that one old woman who had lingered in the kitchen, he had the whole place to himself. There was a good deal of tidying up to do inside his study and he set himself to do it until his keen, handsome face was flushed with the heat of the burning papers. A leather valise stood beside his table, and into this he began to pack very neatly and systematically the precious contents of his safe. He had hardly got started with the work, however, when his quick ears caught the sounds of a distant car. Instantly he gave an exclamation of satisfaction, strapped up the valise, shut the safe, locked it, and hurried out on to the terrace. He was just in time to see the lights of a small car come to a halt at the gate. A passenger sprang out of it and advanced swiftly towards him, while the chauffeur, a heavily built, elderly man with a grey moustache, settled down like one who resigns himself to a long vigil.

'Well?' asked Von Bork eagerly, running forward to meet his visitor.

For answer the man waved a small brown-paper parcel triumphantly above his head.

'You can give me the glad hand tonight, mister,' he cried. 'I'm bringing home the bacon at last.'

'The signals?'

'Same as I said in my cable. Every last one of them, semaphore, lamp code, Marconi – a copy, mind you, not the original. That was too dangerous. But it's the real goods, and you can lay to that.' He slapped the German upon the shoulder with a rough familiarity from which the other winced.

'Come in,' he said. 'I'm all alone in the house. I was only waiting for this. Of course a copy is better than the original. If an original were missing they would change the whole thing. You think it's all safe about the copy?'

The Irish-American had entered the study and stretched his long limbs from the armchair. He was a tall, gaunt man of sixty, with clear-cut features and a small goatee beard which gave him a general resemblance to the caricatures of Uncle Sam. A half-smoked, sodden cigar hung from the corner of his mouth, and as he sat down he struck a match and relit it. 'Making ready for a move?' he remarked as he looked round him. 'Say, mister,' he added, as his eyes fell upon the safe from which the curtain was now removed, 'you don't tell me you keep your papers in that?'

'Why not?'

'Gosh, in a wide-open contraption like that! And they reckon you to be some spy. Why, a Yankee crook would be into that with a can-opener. If I'd known that any letter of mine was goin' to lie loose in a thing like that I'd have been a mug to write to you at all.'

'It would puzzle any crook to force that safe,' Von Bork answered. 'You won't cut that metal with any tool.'

'But the lock?'

'No, it's a double combination lock. You know what that is?'

'Search me,' said the American.

'Well, you need a word as well as a set of figures before you can get the lock to work.' He rose and showed a double-radiating disc round the keyhole. 'This outer one is for the letters, the inner one for the figures.'

'Well, well, that's fine.'

'So it's not quite as simple as you thought. It was four years ago that I had it made, and what do you think I chose for the word and figures?'

'It's beyond me.'

'Well, I chose August for the word, and 1914 for the figures, and here we are.'

The American's face showed his surprise and admiration.

'My, but that was smart! You had it down to a fine thing.'

'Yes, a few of us even then could have guessed the date. Here it is, and I'm shutting down tomorrow morning.'

'Well, I guess you'll have to fix me up also. I'm not staying in this goldarned country all on my lonesome. In a week or less, from what I see, John Bull will be on his hind legs and fair ramping. I'd rather watch him from over the water.'

'But you're an American citizen?'

'Well, so was Jack James an American citizen, but he's doing time in Portland all the same. It cuts no ice with a British copper to tell him you're an American citizen. "It's British law and order over here," says he. By the way, mister, talking of Jack James, it seems to me you don't do much to cover your men.'

'What do you mean?' Von Bork asked sharply.

'Well, you are their employer, ain't you? It's up to you to see that they don't fall down. But they do fall down, and when did you ever pick them up? There's James – '

'It was James's own fault. You know that yourself. He was too self-willed for the job.'

'James was a bonehead – I give you that. Then there was Hollis.'

'The man was mad.'

'Well, he went a bit woozy towards the end. It's enough to make a man bug-house when he has to play a part from morning to night with a hundred guys all ready to set the coppers wise to him. But now there is Steiner – '

Von Bork started violently, and his ruddy face turned a shade paler.

'What about Steiner?'

'Well, they've got him, that's all. They raided his store last night, and he and his papers are all in Portsmouth jail. You'll go off and he, poor devil, will have to stand the racket, and lucky if he gets off with his life. That's why I want to get over the water as soon as you do.'

Von Bork was a strong, self-contained man, but it was easy to see that the news had shaken him.

'How could they have got on to Steiner?' he muttered. 'That's the worst blow yet.'

'Well, you nearly had a worse one, for I believe they are not far off me.'

'You don't mean that!'

'Sure thing. My landlady down Fratton way had some inquiries, and when I heard of it I guessed it was time for me to hustle. But what I want to know, mister, is how the coppers know these things? Steiner is the fifth man you've lost since I signed on with you, and I know the name of the sixth if I don't get a move on. How do you explain it, and ain't you ashamed to see your men go down like this?'

Von Bork flushed crimson.

'How dare you speak in such a way!'

'If I didn't dare things, mister, I wouldn't be in your service. But I'll tell you straight what is in my mind. I've heard that with you German politicians when an agent has done his work you are not sorry to see him put away.'

Von Bork sprang to his feet.

'Do you dare to suggest that I have given away my own agents!'

'I don't stand for that, mister, but there's a stool pigeon or a cross somewhere, and it's up to you to find out where it is. Anyhow I am taking no more chances. It's me for little Holland, and the sooner the better.'

Von Bork had mastered his anger.

'We have been allies too long to quarrel now at the very hour of victory,' he said. 'You've done splendid work and taken risks, and I can't forget it. By all means go to Holland, and you can get a boat from Rotterdam to New York. No other line will be safe a week from now. I'll take that book and pack it with the rest.'

The American held the small parcel in his hand, but made no motion to give it up.

'What about the dough?' he asked.

'The what?'

'The boodle. The reward. The 500 pounds. The

gunner turned damned nasty at the last, and I had to square him with an extra hundred dollars or it would have been nitsky for you and me. "Nothin' doin'!" says he, and he meant it, too, but the last hundred did it. It's cost me two hundred pound from first to last, so it isn't likely I'd give it up without gettin' my wad.'

Von Bork smiled with some bitterness. 'You don't seem to have a very high opinion of my honour,' said he, 'you want the money before you give up the book.'

'Well, mister, it is a business proposition.'

'All right. Have your way.' He sat down at the table and scribbled a cheque, which he tore from the book, but he refrained from handing it to his companion. 'After all, since we are to be on such terms, Mr. Altamont,' said he, 'I don't see why I should trust you any more than you trust me. Do you understand?' he added, looking back over his shoulder at the American. 'There's the cheque upon the table. I claim the right to examine that parcel before you pick the money up.'

The American passed it over without a word. Von Bork undid a winding of string and two wrappers of paper. Then he sat gazing for a moment in silent amazement at a small blue book which lay before him. Across the cover was printed in golden letters Practical Handbook of Bee Culture. Only for one instant did the master spy glare at this strangely irrelevant inscription. The next he was gripped at the back of his neck by a grasp of iron, and a chloroformed sponge was held in front of his writhing face.

'Another glass, Watson!' said Mr. Sherlock Holmes as he extended the bottle of Imperial Tokay.

The thickset chauffeur, who had seated himself by the table, pushed forward his glass with some eagerness.

'It is a good wine, Holmes.'

'A remarkable wine, Watson. Our friend upon the sofa has assured me that it is from Franz Josef's special cellar at the Schoenbrunn Palace. Might I trouble you to open the window, for chloroform vapour does not help the palate.'

The safe was ajar, and Holmes standing in front of it was removing dossier after dossier, swiftly examining each, and then packing it neatly in Von Bork's valise. The German lay upon the sofa sleeping stertorously with a strap round his upper arms and another round his legs.

'We need not hurry ourselves, Watson. We are safe from interruption. Would you mind touching the bell? There is no one in the house except old Martha, who has played her part to admiration. I got her the situation here when first I took the matter up. Ah, Martha, you will be glad to hear that all is well.'

The pleasant old lady had appeared in the doorway.

She curtseyed with a smile to Mr. Holmes, but glanced with some apprehension at the figure upon the sofa.

'It is all right, Martha. He has not been hurt at all.'

'I am glad of that, Mr. Holmes. According to his lights he has been a kind master. He wanted me to go with his wife to Germany yesterday, but that would hardly have suited your plans, would it, sir?'

'No, indeed, Martha. So long as you were here I was easy in my mind. We waited some time for your signal tonight.'

'It was the secretary, sir.'

'I know. His car passed ours.'

'I thought he would never go. I knew that it would not suit your plans, sir, to find him here.'

'No, indeed. Well, it only meant that we waited half an hour or so until I saw your lamp go out and knew that the coast was clear. You can report to me tomorrow in London, Martha, at Claridge's Hotel.'

'Very good, sir.'

'I suppose you have everything ready to leave.'

'Yes, sir. He posted seven letters today. I have the addresses as usual.'

'Very good, Martha. I will look into them tomorrow. Goodnight. These papers,' he continued as the old lady vanished, 'are not of very great importance, for, of course, the information which they represent has been sent off long ago to the German government.

These are the originals which could not safely be got out of the country.'

'Then they are of no use.'

'I should not go so far as to say that, Watson. They will at least show our people what is known and what is not. I may say that a good many of these papers have come through me, and I need not add are thoroughly untrustworthy. It would brighten my declining years to see a German cruiser navigating the Solent according to the mine-field plans which I have furnished. But you, Watson' – he stopped his work and took his old friend by the shoulders – 'I've hardly seen you in the light yet. How have the years used you? You look the same blithe boy as ever.'

'I feel twenty years younger, Holmes. I have seldom felt so happy as when I got your wire asking me to meet you at Harwich with the car. But you, Holmes – you have changed very little – save for that horrible goatee.'

'These are the sacrifices one makes for one's country, Watson,' said Holmes, pulling at his little tuft. 'Tomorrow it will be but a dreadful memory. With my hair cut and a few other superficial changes I shall no doubt reappear at Claridge's tomorrow as I was before this American stunt – I beg your pardon, Watson, my well of English seems to be permanently defiled – before this American job came my way.'

'But you have retired, Holmes. We heard of you as living the life of a hermit among your bees and your books in a small farm upon the South Downs.'

'Exactly, Watson. Here is the fruit of my leisured ease, the magnum opus of my latter years!' He picked up the volume from the table and read out the whole title, Practical Handbook of Bee Culture, with Some Observations upon the Segregation of the Queen. 'Alone I did it. Behold the fruit of pensive nights and laborious days when I watched the little working gangs as once I watched the criminal world of London.'

'But how did you get to work again?'

'Ah, I have often marvelled at it myself. The Foreign Minister alone I could have withstood, but when the Premier also deigned to visit my humble roof – ! The fact is, Watson, that this gentleman upon the sofa was a bit too good for our people. He was in a class by himself. Things were going wrong, and no one could understand why they were going wrong. Agents were suspected or even caught, but there was evidence of some strong and secret central force. It was absolutely necessary to expose it. Strong pressure was brought upon me to look into the matter. It has cost me two years, Watson, but they have not been devoid of excitement. When I say that I started my pilgrimage at Chicago, graduated in an Irish secret society at Buffalo, gave serious trouble to the constabulary at

Skibbareen, and so eventually caught the eye of a subordinate agent of Von Bork, who recommended me as a likely man, you will realise that the matter was complex. Since then I have been honoured by his confidence, which has not prevented most of his plans going subtly wrong and five of his best agents being in prison. I watched them, Watson, and I picked them as they ripened. Well, sir, I hope that you are none the worse!'

The last remark was addressed to Von Bork himself, who after much gasping and blinking had lain quietly listening to Holmes's statement. He broke out now into a furious stream of German invective, his face convulsed with passion. Holmes continued his swift investigation of documents while his prisoner cursed and swore.

'Though unmusical, German is the most expressive of all languages,' he observed when Von Bork had stopped from pure exhaustion. 'Hullo! Hullo!' he added as he looked hard at the corner of a tracing before putting it in the box. 'This should put another bird in the cage. I had no idea that the paymaster was such a rascal, though I have long had an eye upon him. Mister Von Bork, you have a great deal to answer for.'

The prisoner had raised himself with some difficulty upon the sofa and was staring with a strange mixture of amazement and hatred at his captor.

'I shall get level with you, Altamont,' he said, speaking with slow deliberation. 'If it takes me all my life I shall get level with you!'

'The old sweet song,' said Holmes. 'How often have I heard it in days gone by. It was a favourite ditty of the late lamented Professor Moriarty. Colonel Sebastian Moran has also been known to warble it. And yet I live and keep bees upon the South Downs.'

'Curse you, you double traitor!' cried the German, straining against his bonds and glaring murder from his furious eyes.

'No, no, it is not so bad as that,' said Holmes, smiling. 'As my speech surely shows you, Mr. Altamont of Chicago had no existence in fact. I used him and he is gone.'

'Then who are you?'

'It is really immaterial who I am, but since the matter seems to interest you, Mr. Von Bork, I may say that this is not my first acquaintance with the members of your family. I have done a good deal of business in Germany in the past and my name is probably familiar to you.'

'I would wish to know it,' said the Prussian grimly.

'It was I who brought about the separation between Irene Adler and the late King of Bohemia when your cousin Heinrich was the Imperial Envoy. It was I also who saved from murder, by the Nihilist Klopman,

Count Von und Zu Grafenstein, who was your mother's elder brother. It was I – '

Von Bork sat up in amazement.

'There is only one man,' he cried.

'Exactly,' said Holmes.

Von Bork groaned and sank back on the sofa. 'And most of that information came through you,' he cried. 'What is it worth? What have I done? It is my ruin forever!'

'It is certainly a little untrustworthy,' said Holmes. 'It will require some checking and you have little time to check it. Your admiral may find the new guns rather larger than he expects, and the cruisers perhaps a trifle faster.'

Von Bork clutched at his own throat in despair.

'There are a good many other points of detail which will, no doubt, come to light in good time. But you have one quality which is very rare in a German, Mr. Von Bork: you are a sportsman and you will bear me no ill-will when you realise that you, who have outwitted so many other people, have at last been outwitted yourself. After all, you have done your best for your country, and I have done my best for mine, and what could be more natural? Besides,' he added, not unkindly, as he laid his hand upon the shoulder of the prostrate man, 'it is better than to fall before some ignoble foe. These papers are now ready, Watson. If you will help me with our prisoner, I think that we may get started for London at once.'

It was no easy task to move Von Bork, for he was a strong and a desperate man. Finally, holding either arm, the two friends walked him very slowly down the garden walk which he had trod with such proud confidence when he received the congratulations of the famous diplomatist only a few hours before. After a short, final struggle he was hoisted, still bound hand and foot, into the spare seat of the little car. His precious valise was wedged in beside him.

'I trust that you are as comfortable as circumstances permit,' said Holmes when the final arrangements were made. 'Should I be guilty of a liberty if I lit a cigar and placed it between your lips?'

But all amenities were wasted upon the angry German.

'I suppose you realise, Mr. Sherlock Holmes,' said he, 'that if your government bears you out in this treatment it becomes an act of war.'

'What about your government and all this treatment?' said Holmes, tapping the valise.

'You are a private individual. You have no warrant for my arrest. The whole proceeding is absolutely illegal and outrageous.'

'Absolutely,' said Holmes.

'Kidnapping a German subject.'

'And stealing his private papers.'

'Well, you realise your position, you and your accomplice here. If I were to shout for help as we pass through the village –'

'My dear sir, if you did anything so foolish you would probably enlarge the two limited titles of our village inns by giving us "The Dangling Prussian" as a signpost. The Englishman is a patient creature, but at present his temper is a little inflamed, and it would be as well not to try him too far. No, Mr. Von Bork, you will go with us in a quiet, sensible fashion to Scotland Yard, whence you can send for your friend, Baron Von Herling, and see if even now you may not fill that place which he has reserved for you in the ambassadorial suite. As to you, Watson, you are joining us with your old service, as I understand, so London won't be out of your way. Stand with me here upon the terrace, for it may be the last quiet talk that we shall ever have.'

The two friends chatted in intimate converse for a few minutes, recalling once again the days of the past, while their prisoner vainly wriggled to undo the bonds that held him. As they turned to the car Holmes pointed back to the moonlit sea and shook a thoughtful head.

'There's an east wind coming, Watson.'

'I think not, Holmes. It is very warm.'

'Good old Watson! You are the one fixed point in a changing age. There's an east wind coming all the same, such a wind as never blew on England yet. It will be cold and bitter, Watson, and a good many of us may wither before its blast. But it's God's own wind none the less, and a cleaner, better, stronger land will lie in the sunshine when the storm has cleared. Start her up, Watson, for it's time that we were on our way. I have a cheque for five hundred pounds which should be cashed early, for the drawer is quite capable of stopping it if he can.'

# INTRODUCTION

'A Place on the Piano', Eva Ibbotson
'Swept and Garnished', Rudyard Kipling

Rudyard Kipling was one of the most famous authors of his day, loved for his children's stories and also his depictions of the British Empire. At the outbreak of the First World War, Kipling was a fierce believer that the British must fight, and much of his writing at this time took the form of war propaganda. 'Swept and Garnished' uses the horrible image of children displaced and injured at the hands of the enemy to prompt readers to take up arms and retaliate.

Eva Ibbotson's story deals with another child who has been made orphan and homeless by war. In a grand gesture, a wealthy English family decide to retrieve and adopt the child, but when she is found she has already been saved.

What reactions do you think the authors want people back home to have to these stories?

# A PLACE ON THE PIANO

## Eva Ibbotson

I always thought the war would end suddenly but it didn't – it sort of dribbled away. Six months after I stood with the other boys in my class outside Buckingham Palace – yelling for the king and queen because we'd defeated Hitler – the barrage balloons still floated like great silver grandfathers over the roofs of London. The park railings were still missing, St Paul's cathedral stood in a sea of rubble and there was nothing to be bought in the shops.

My teacher had explained it to me. 'Wars are expensive, Michael,' he said. 'They have to be paid for.'

Rationing got tighter – you still had to have coupons for clothes and fuel. Worst of all was the food. You could hardly see the meat ration with the naked eye, and some very weird things were issued by the government for us to eat. Tinned snoek, for example. Snoek is a South African fish and when Cook opened the tin it turned out to be a bluish animal with terrifying spikes, swimming in a sea of gelatinous goo – and the smell was unspeakable.

'This time they've gone too far,' she said, and she tried to give it to the cat, who sneered and turned away.

I knew quite a lot about rationing because I was a sort of kitchen boy. Not that I worked in the kitchen exactly; I'd just won a scholarship to the grammar school, but I lived below stairs in the basement of a large house belonging to a family called Glossop, where my mother was the housekeeper. We'd lived there, in London, all through the war.

I remember the snoek particularly because we were just wondering what to do with it when the bell went and my mother was called upstairs.

When she came back she looked really happy and excited. 'Little Marianne Gerstenberger has been found. She's alive!'

It was incredible news. Marianne had been thrown out of a cattle train when she was a baby. It was her own mother who had done it. She'd been rounded up with some other Jews and she was on her way to a concentration camp when she found a weak place in one of the boards behind the latrine. She got the others to help her work on it to make a small hole. And then she bundled up the baby, and when the train stopped for a moment she managed to push her out on to the track.

We'd heard a lot about bravery during the last six years of war: soldiers in Burma stumbling on, dying of thirst; parachutists at Arnheim, and of course the Spitfire pilots who had saved us in the Blitz. But the story of Marianne caught us all.

'To do that,' said my mother, 'to push your own baby out on to the track because you knew you were going to your death ...'

At first my mother had tried not to speak of what had happened when Hitler went mad and tried to exterminate the Jews. But my school was the kind where they told you things, and I'd seen the newsreels. I'd seen the bodies piled up when the Allies opened up the camps, and the skeletons which were supposed to be people. Marianne's parents had both perished, but now, as the news came through from the Red Cross in Switzerland, it seemed that the baby had survived. She had been found by a peasant family who had taken her in and was living in East Germany, close to the border with Poland.

'They're going to fetch her,' said my mother. 'They're going to take her in.' And there were tears in her eyes.

'They' were her employers – the Glossops – who lived in the house above us and who she served. The Glossops were not Jewish, but Marianne's mother had been married to the son of their Jewish business partners in Berlin. Glossop and Gerstenberger had been a well-known firm of exporters.

'They're going to adopt her,' my mother went on. She didn't often speak warmly about the Glossops, but I could hear the admiration in her voice.

'She'll live like a little princess,' said Cook. 'Imagine, after being brought up with peasants.'

Everyone agreed with this: the kids in my school, the people in the shops, the tradesmen who came to deliver goods to the basement. Because the Glossops weren't just well off, they were properly rich. Their house was the largest in the square, double-fronted – and furnished as though the war had never been. To go up the service stairs and through the green baize door into the house was like stepping into a different world.

Mrs Glossop and her mother-in-law had spent the war in a hotel in the Lake District to get away from the bombs; and her daughter, Daphne, who was ten years old, had been away at boarding school, but the house had stayed open because Mr Glossop used it when he was in town on business, which meant that the servants had to keep it ready for him whenever he wanted.

So my mother and I went upstairs most days to check the blackout curtains and make sure the shutters were closed and none of the window panes had cracked in the raids – and I knew the house as well as I knew the dark rooms in the basement where we lived, along with the cook and old Tom, the chauffeur-handyman.

I knew the dining room with its heavy button-backed chairs and the carved sideboard where they kept the napkin rings and the cruets which Tom polished every week. I knew the drawing room with its thick Turkish carpet and massive sofas – and I knew old Mrs Glossop's boudoir on the first floor with the gilt mirrors and clawfooted tables – and the piano.

I knew the piano very well. I remember once when I was upstairs helping my mother I heard a V1 rocket cut out above me, which meant I had about half a minute before it came down and exploded – and without thinking I dived under the piano.

It was an enormous piano – a Steinway Concert Grand – but I'd never heard anybody play it. It was a piano for keeping relations on. On the dark red chenille cover which protected it were rows of Glossops in silver frames: old Glossops and young ones, Glossops on their horses and Glossops in their university gowns. There were Glossop children in their school uniforms or holding cricket bats, and there were Glossop women in their presentation dresses ready to go to court. There was even a Glossop who had been knighted, and as I lay there, waiting for the bomb to fall, I wasn't in the least bit scared – I didn't feel anyone would dare to destroy a whole army of Glossops, and I was right. The rocket came down three streets away.

And now Marianne Gerstenberger, who was just seven years old, would have her own place on the piano, and be a Glossop too.

The preparations for Marianne began straightaway, and we all threw ourselves into the work. It may sound silly, but I think it was then that we realized that the war was well and truly over, and that good things were happening in the world.

'We'll put her in the room next to Daphne's,' said Mrs Glossop – and she gave my mother a list of all the things that needed to be done. New curtains of pale blue satin to be sewn, and the bed canopied with the same material. A white fur rug on the floor, the walls repapered with a design of forget-me-nots and rosebuds, and a new dressing table to be lined with a matching pattern. Furniture was difficult to get – you had to have coupons for almost everything – but when you own three department stores the rules don't really apply. The Glossops had always had everything they wanted, and that included food. Parcels from America had come all through the war and they were coming still.

'She can have my dolls – I don't play with them any more,' said Daphne, but Mrs Glossop ordered a whole batch of new dolls and fluffy toys and games from the store.

'Of course she'll be a little savage,' said old Mrs Glossop. 'We must be patient with her.'

She sent my mother out to get one of the napkin rings engraved with Marianne's name and I imagined the little girl sitting in the big solemn dining room with all the Glossop ancestors looking down from the wall, carefully rolling up her damask napkin after every meal.

Actually, I knew exactly the sort of life Marianne was going to lead, because of Daphne.

Daphne didn't speak to me much; she was not the sort of girl who spoke to servants. A year earlier I'd pulled off an Alsatian who was holding her at bay as she played in the gardens of the square, and got quite badly bitten, and while my hands were bandaged she was positively friendly, but it didn't last.

Mostly Daphne was away at boarding school, but when she was at home she led a very busy life. On Saturday morning she put on her jodhpurs and Tom drove her to the park where she went riding – trotting down the sanded paths and greeting other children on well-groomed ponies. On Monday afternoon, she carried her dancing shoes in a velvet bag to Miss Bigelow's Academy and learned ballet, and on Thursdays she did elocution with a lady called Madame Farnari.

Marianne would do all this – but not for long, because as soon as she had her eighth birthday she would be taken to a school outfitter to buy a brown velour hat and a brown gymslip and a hockey stick and go off with Daphne to St Hilda's, where the school motto was 'Play straight and play the game'.

'When you think what that school costs, and the kind of children who go there – all those honourables and what have you – it'll be a wonderful thing for the little thing,' said old Tom, the chauffeur. 'Mind you, she'll have a lot to learn.'

As it turned out, we had several months to get ready for Marianne, because even the Glossops didn't find it easy to get the passports and permits and papers that were needed to bring Marianne to Britain. Things were made more difficult because the village where Marianne now lived was in the part of Germany that was occupied by the Russians and they were very strict about who could come into their zone and who could not.

But at last a permit came through, allowing two people to travel to Orthausen and pick up the little girl. The permit was for a particular week in July and now my mother was sent for again. What's more, she was asked to sit down, which was unusual.

'It's so awkward, such a nuisance,' said Mrs Glossop to my mother. 'But the permit covers the day of the royal garden party and I've been asked to attend. I simply couldn't miss that – and two days later it's Daphne's prize-giving at St Hilda's and of course I must go down for that.'

My mother waited, wondering why she had been summoned.

'My husband would go and fetch the little girl, but he has the annual meeting of the cricket club and then a very important Rotary dinner in Aberdeen at which he's been asked to speak.' She bent forward and fixed my mother with a stern eye. 'So I want you to fetch Marianne. It's so convenient because you speak German.'

This was true. My mother had been studying modern languages at university when my father had married and deserted her, all in three months.

But my mother said she couldn't leave me. This was nonsense, of course, but she said it very firmly. I think she felt that the Glossops should go themselves to fetch their new daughter – or perhaps she was nervous. Since my father betrayed her, she had looked for a quiet life – a life where the two of us would be safe.

'Well, the permit is for two people. I don't see why Michael shouldn't go with you; we don't have to say that he's only twelve years old.'

So it was my mother and I who went to fetch Marianne Gerstenberger, but before we left we were given some very important instructions.

'Marianne has a birthmark on her arm,' said Mrs Glossop. 'Her mother wrote to us about it when she was born. It's on her right arm and it runs from her shoulder to her elbow – and you must make absolutely sure that she does have that mark and in the right place. It's one thing to adopt the daughter of one's husband's partner and another to take in any stray that wants a comfortable home.' And she told us that though Marianne's name had been pinned to her blanket, it was possible that in those frightful times the baby's things had been stolen and given to some other child.

'We will make sure,' promised my mother – and two weeks later we set off.

It was quite a journey. Ordinary people hadn't been allowed to travel all through the war and of course I was excited, crossing the Channel, getting a train to go through the Netherlands and Germany.

Or rather, five trains. Most of the rolling stock had been destroyed in Allied bombing raids. We stopped and started and were pushed out on to the platform and back in again. There was no food to be had on the train, or water, and I couldn't help wondering if it was because she knew how uncomfortable the journey was going to be that Mrs Glossop had decided to send my mother instead. We went through towns that were nothing but heaps of rubble and countryside with burnt and empty fields. It was odd to think that it was we who had caused all this destruction. I'd thought of bombing as something that the Germans did.

We spent the night in a cold and gloomy little hotel on the Belgian border, and the next day we travelled east through Germany.

I asked my mother if this was the route that Marianne's mother would have travelled on her last journey but she didn't know.

We were going through farmland now: fields and copses and little villages. The houses looked poor and small but there were a few animals: cows and sheep. The peasants were struggling to get back to a normal life.

We had to change twice more on to branch lines, travelling on trains so old that we didn't think they would manage to pull their loads. Then in the late afternoon we reached Orthausen.

The village that Marianne lived in was not directly on the railway. The woman who found her must have carried her bundle a long way to her house. My mother and I now walked that road, trudging along the white dust village street with our bags and turning off along a track which ran beside a stream.

Then, late in the afternoon, we crossed a small bridge and came to a wooden house standing by itself in a clearing.

Marianne was sitting on the steps of the porch. She was holding a tortoiseshell kitten on her lap and talking to it – not fussing over it, just telling it to behave. She spoke in German, but I knew exactly what she was saying.

She had thick, fawn, curly hair and brown eyes and she wore a dirndl, and over it a knitted jersey which covered her arms. When she saw us she put down the kitten and then she reached for the bag my mother carried and led us into the house.

The woman who had found Marianne on the railway track was called Mrs Wasilewski. She was very pale with a screwed-down bun of fair hair and a tight mouth. To me she looked like a death's head, so white and forbidding, and I was glad that we were going to take Marianne away from such a cold, stern woman. But Marianne went up to her trustingly and said, here were the visitors from England, and I realized that she did not yet know why we had come.

Mrs Wasilewski offered us some ersatz coffee and slices of dark bread spread with dripping. Her husband was away, working in a sawmill in the north of the country for the summer, to earn some extra money. When we had eaten, Marianne turned to me and took me by the hand, and said, '*Komm*,' and I got up and followed her.

When somebody takes you by the hand and says '*Komm*', it is not difficult to guess what they are saying, but it still seems odd to me that the first moment I understood Marianne so completely, and that she understood me.

The Wasilewskis had a smallholding, but the Germans had commandeered the horse at the beginning of the war and the Russians had taken the cow at the end of it. All the same, the animals that were left seemed to satisfy Marianne. She introduced me to the two goats – a white one, called Bella, and a bad-tempered brown one, called Sidonia, after a disagreeable lady who scowled at everybody in the church. She showed me the five hens and told me their names and the rabbits and the new piglet, honking in the straw.

Actually, it was more than showing – she sort of presented them to me, giving me the animals to hold as if hanging on to a squawking chicken or a lop-eared rabbit must make me the happiest person in the world.

It was far too late to try and make our way back that night – no one knew how the trains would run. Mrs Wasilewski – still unsmiling and gaunt – led us to a loft with two goose-down duvets on a slatted wooden board and we went to bed.

I was sure we'd leave the next morning, but we didn't. My mother helped Mrs Wasilewski with the housework and once again Marianne put out her hand and said, '*Komm*,' and once again I came.

She led me to a part of the stream where the water ran clear over a bed of pebbles. Both of us took off our shoes, but she kept on her jersey, and we walked along the river bed, dredging up bright and glittering stones.

'*Nicht Gold*,' she said, holding out a yellow-veined stone and shaking her head, but she was smiling. She didn't want gold, I could see that. She wanted brightness.

The stream was full of sticklebacks and newts and tiny frogs; all the creatures too small to have been stolen or pillaged in war.

After a while a boy and a girl appeared – a brother and sister – and Marianne introduced me, carefully pronouncing my name in the English way I'd taught her.

We came to a bridge where the current ran quite fast and we each chose a stick and raced it from one side to the other. I hadn't done that since I was at infant school, but you can't go wrong with Pooh sticks, and I found myself wondering if they played it at St Hilda's.

Mrs Wasilewski, still grim and silent, gave us lunch – pieces of salt bacon with beetroot and cabbage from her garden – and afterwards Marianne took me out and showed me the rows of vegetables, and picked a pea pod from the vine and opened it, dropping the shelled peas into my palm.

All that day Marianne stretched out her hand and said, '*Komm.*' She showed me a hedgehog asleep in the potting shed and a place where raspberries grew wild, and I made her a whistle out of a hazel twig. I'd brought my Swiss Army knife, and the whistle was a good one. They don't always work but this one did.

Even the next day my mother said nothing about leaving. We slept on the floor; the work she was helping with was far harder than any that she did in England and Mrs Wasilewski still went round like a zombie, but my mother didn't seem in any hurry to return.

That day Marianne showed me her special tree. It was an ancient oak standing on its own on a small hill and it was the kind of tree that is a whole world in itself. There were hollows in the trunk where squirrels had stored their nuts; beetles sheltered under the bark and a woodpecker tapped in the branches.

Marianne had not *built* a tree-house because the

tree *was* her house. She explained this as we climbed up – and that it was in this house that she kept her treasures. They lived in a tin with a picture of cough lozenges on the lid, and she showed them to me, one by one. There was a tortoiseshell hair slide, a little bent; a bracelet made out of glass beads; a propelling pencil – and her most important possession: a small bear, carved roughly out of wood, which Mr Wasilweski had made on her last birthday. Then she took the whistle I had made for her out of her pocket and laid it carefully in the tin beside the other things, and closed the lid.

But the best thing about the tree was the view. Because it stood on a knoll you could see the surrounding countryside for miles. Marianne pointed to a small farm and told me that the man who had lived there had been killed on the Eastern Front. He'd been a German, of course – maybe a Nazi – but Marianne's face grew sad as she told me about him, which was strange because her mother's people had been so horribly persecuted by men like him.

If she was the child we thought she was …

But in the opposite direction was a low, red-roofed house and she told me that the man who owned it had a litter of sheepdog puppies and he was going to let her have one. There was enough food now to keep a dog, she said joyfully; it was no longer forbidden.

I didn't say anything. She would never be able to bring a dog into England; the quarantine regulations were far too strict, and the Glossops said it wasn't fair to keep animals in town. Even the cat we kept in the basement knew better than to make her way upstairs.

Then on the morning of the third day my mother called me into the kitchen. Mrs Wasilewski was there, more silent and morose than ever. There was a bundle on the table: the blanket Marianne had been wrapped in, I guessed, when she was found on the track, and a few baby clothes. Mrs Wasilweski called Marianne to her side and she came. For the first time, she looked puzzled and anxious.

'Wait,' said my mother. 'We must make sure we have the right child.' And very gently she said, 'Will you take your jersey off, Marianne, and your blouse?'

Marianne looked at Mrs Wasilewski, who nodded. Then she took off her jersey and undid the drawstring of her blouse.

Now she stood before us with both arms bare. From her shoulder to her elbow, her right arm was covered in a dark brown birthmark.

It was exactly what the Glossops had described to us. Without a doubt, the child who stood before us was the child who had been thrown from the train.

My mother and I looked at each other. Mrs Wasilewski stood like a ramrod, her mouth tight shut.

Marianne, still puzzled, reached for her blouse and began to put it on.

The room was very still. Then my mother cleared her throat and looked at me again. She looked at me hard.

'What a pity,' she said clearly to Mrs Wasilewski. 'I'm so sorry. I'm afraid this is the wrong child. We can't take her back with us – her birthmark is on the wrong arm.' And then, softly: 'She will have to stay with you.'

The silence was broken suddenly by a gasp – followed by a kind of juddering sound. Then Mrs Wasilewski went mad. Her head dropped forward on to the table and she began to cry – but you can't call it crying. She erupted in tears, she became completely drenched in them, her hair came down and fell in damp strands across the table. I have never in all my life heard anybody cry like that.

When she lifted her head again she was a totally different woman; she was rosy, she laughed, she hugged my mother and me. And I understood what my mother had understood at once – that this woman who had made Marianne's world with such loving care had been almost destroyed at the thought of losing her.

In the train my mother said, 'I think we'll just say there was no birthmark. We don't want any further fuss about left or right.'

'Yes.' The train chugged on through what had once been enemy territory and was now just the great plain of central Europe. 'I'm going back,' I said. 'Later.' And then: 'Not much later.'

'Yes, I know,' said my mother. 'And I'm going on.'

(And she did too. She gave up her job with the Glossops and went back to finish her degree. We lived in two small rooms and were very happy.)

When we got back we were called up to the boudoir so that the old lady too could hear our story.

'Oh, well,' said Mrs Glossop, when we'd finished. 'It's a pity, when we had so much to offer a child. But it doesn't sound as though she would have fitted in.'

And my mother looked at the piano, with its two dozen important Glossops in silver frames, and said no, she wouldn't have fitted in. She wouldn't have fitted in at all.

# SWEPT AND GARNISHED

## Rudyard Kipling

When the first waves of feverish cold stole over Frau Ebermann, she very wisely telephoned for the doctor and went to bed. He diagnosed the attack as mild influenza, prescribed the appropriate remedies, and left her to the care of her one servant in her comfortable Berlin flat. Frau Ebermann, beneath the thick coverlet, curled up with what patience she could until the aspirin should begin to act, and Anna should come back from the chemist with the formamint, the ammoniated quinine, the eucalyptus, and the little tin steam-inhaler. Meantime, every bone in her body ached; her head throbbed; her hot, dry hands would not stay the same size for a minute together; and her body, tucked into the smallest possible compass, shrank from the chill of the well-warmed sheets.

Of a sudden she noticed that an imitation-lace cover which should have lain mathematically square with the imitation-marble top of the radiator behind the green plush sofa had slipped away so that one corner hung over the bronze-painted steam pipes. She recalled that she must have rested her poor head against the radiator-top while she was taking off her boots. She tried to get up and set the thing straight, but the radiator at once receded toward the horizon, which, unlike true horizons, slanted diagonally, exactly parallel with the dropped lace edge of the cover. Frau Ebermann groaned through sticky lips and lay still.

'Certainly, I have a temperature,' she said. 'Certainly, I have a grave temperature. I should have been warned by that chill after dinner.'

She resolved to shut her hot-lidded eyes, but opened them in a little while to torture herself with the knowledge of that ungeometrical thing against the far wall. Then she saw a child – an untidy, thin-faced little girl of about ten, who must have strayed in from the adjoining flat. This proved – Frau Ebermann groaned again at the way the world falls to bits when one is sick – proved that Anna had forgotten to shut the outer door of the flat when she went to the chemist. Frau Ebermann had had children of her own, but they were all grown up now, and she had never been a child-lover in any sense. Yet the intruder might be made to serve her scheme of things.

'Make – put,' she muttered thickly, 'that white thing straight on the top of that yellow thing.'

The child paid no attention, but moved about the room, investigating everything that came in her way – the yellow cut-glass handles of the chest of drawers, the stamped bronze hook to hold back the heavy puce curtains, and the mauve enamel, New Art finger-plates on the door. Frau Ebermann watched indignantly.

'Aie! That is bad and rude. Go away!' she cried, though it hurt her to raise her voice. 'Go away by the road you came!' The child passed behind the bed-foot, where she could not see her. 'Shut the door as you go. I will speak to Anna, but – first, put that white thing straight.'

She closed her eyes in misery of body and soul. The outer door clicked, and Anna entered, very penitent that she had stayed so long at the chemist's. But it had been difficult to find the proper type of inhaler, and –

'Where did the child go?' moaned Frau Ebermann – 'the child that was here?'

'There was no child,' said startled Anna. 'How should any child come in when I shut the door behind me after I go out? All the keys of the flats are different.'

'No, no! You forgot this time. But my back is aching, and up my legs also. Besides, who knows what it may have fingered and upset? Look and see.'

'Nothing is fingered, nothing is upset,' Anna replied, as she took the inhaler from its paper box.

'Yes, there is. Now I remember all about it. Put – put that white thing, with the open edge – the lace, I mean – quite straight on that – ' she pointed. Anna, accustomed to her ways, understood and went to it.

'Now, is it quite straight?' Frau Ebermann demanded.

'Perfectly,' said Anna. 'In fact, in the very centre of the radiator.' Anna measured the equal margins with her knuckle, as she had been told to do when she first took service.

'And my tortoise-shell hair brushes?' Frau Ebermann could not command her dressing-table from where she lay.

'Perfectly straight, side by side in the big tray, and the comb laid across them. Your watch also in the coralline watch-holder. Everything' – she moved round the room to make sure – 'everything is as you have it when you are well.' Frau Ebermann sighed with relief. It seemed to her that the room and her head had suddenly grown cooler.

'Good!' said she. 'Now warm my night-gown in the kitchen, so it will be ready when I have perspired. And the towels also. Make the inhaler steam, and put in the eucalyptus; that is good for the larynx. Then sit you in the kitchen, and come when I ring. But, first, my hot-water bottle.'

It was brought and scientifically tucked in.

'What news?' said Frau Ebermann drowsily. She had not been out that day.

'Another victory,' said Anna. 'Many more prisoners and guns.'

Frau Ebermann purred, one might almost say grunted, contentedly.

'That is good too,' she said; and Anna, after lighting the inhaler-lamp, went out.

Frau Ebermann reflected that in an hour or so the aspirin would begin to work, and all would be well. Tomorrow – no, the day after – she would take up life with something to talk over with her friends at coffee. It was rare – everyone knew it – that she should be overcome by any ailment. Yet in all her distresses she had not allowed the minutest deviation from daily routine and ritual. She would tell her friends – she ran over their names one by one – exactly what measures she had taken against the lace cover on the radiator-top and in regard to her two tortoise-shell hair brushes and the comb at right angles. How she had set everything in order – everything in order. She roved further afield as she wriggled her toes luxuriously on the hot-water bottle. If it pleased our dear God to take her to Himself, and she was not so young as she had been – there was that plate of the four lower ones in the blue tooth-glass, for instance – He should find all her belongings fit to meet His eye.

'Swept and garnished' were the words that shaped themselves in her intent brain. 'Swept and garnished for – '

No, it was certainly not for the dear Lord that she had swept; she would have her room swept out tomorrow or the day after, and garnished. Her hands began to swell again into huge pillows of nothingness. Then they shrank, and so did her head, to minute dots. It occurred to her that she was waiting for some event, some tremendously important event, to come to pass. She lay with shut eyes for a long time till her head and hands should return to their proper size.

She opened her eyes with a jerk.

'How stupid of me,' she said aloud, 'to set the room in order for a parcel of dirty little children!'

They were there – five of them, two little boys and three girls – headed by the anxious-eyed ten-year-old whom she had seen before. They must have entered by the outer door, which Anna had neglected to shut behind her when she returned with the inhaler. She counted them backward and forward as one counts scales – one, two, three, four, five.

They took no notice of her, but hung about, first on one foot then on the other, like strayed chickens, the smaller ones holding by the larger. They had the air of utterly wearied passengers in a railway waiting-room, and their clothes were disgracefully dirty.

'Go away!' cried Frau Ebermann at last, after she had struggled, it seemed to her, for years to shape the words.

'You called?' said Anna at the living-room door.

'No,' said her mistress. 'Did you shut the flat door when you came in?'

'Assuredly,' said Anna. 'Besides, it is made to catch shut of itself.'

'Then go away,' said she, very little above a whisper. If Anna pretended not to see the children, she would speak to Anna later on.

'And now,' she said, turning toward them as soon as the door closed. The smallest of the crowd smiled at her, and shook his head before he buried it in his sister's skirts.

'Why – don't – you – go – away?' she whispered earnestly.

Again they took no notice, but, guided by the elder girl, set themselves to climb, boots and all, on to the green plush sofa in front of the radiator. The little boys had to be pushed, as they could not compass the stretch unaided. They settled themselves in a row, with small gasps of relief, and pawed the plush approvingly.

'I ask you – I ask you why do you not go away – why do you not go away?' Frau Ebermann found herself repeating the question twenty times. It seemed to her that everything in the world hung on the answer. 'You know you should not come into houses and rooms unless you are invited. Not houses and bedrooms, you know.'

'No,' a solemn little six-year-old repeated, 'not houses nor bedrooms, nor dining-rooms, nor churches, nor all those places. Shouldn't come in. It's rude.'

'Yes, he said so,' the younger girl put in proudly. 'He said it. He told them only pigs would do that.' The line nodded and dimpled one to another with little explosive giggles, such as children use when they tell deeds of great daring against their elders.

'If you know it is wrong, that makes it much worse,' said Frau Ebermann.

'Oh yes; much worse,' they assented cheerfully, till the smallest boy changed his smile to a baby wail of weariness.

'When will they come for us?' he asked, and the girl at the head of the row hauled him bodily into her square little capable lap.

'He's tired,' she explained. 'He is only four. He only had his first breeches this spring.' They came almost under his armpits, and were held up by broad linen braces, which, his sorrow diverted for the moment, he patted proudly.

'Yes, beautiful, dear,' said both girls.

'Go away!' said Frau Ebermann. 'Go home to your father and mother!'

Their faces grew grave at once.

'H'sh! We *can't*,' whispered the eldest. 'There isn't anything left.'

'All gone,' a boy echoed, and he puffed through pursed lips. 'Like *that*, uncle told me. Both cows too.'

'And my own three ducks,' the boy on the girl's lap said sleepily.

'So, you see, we came here.' The elder girl leaned forward a little, caressing the child she rocked.

'I – I don't understand,' said Frau Ebermann. 'Are you lost, then? You must tell our police.'

'Oh no; we are only waiting.'

'But what are you waiting *for?*'

'We are waiting for our people to come for us. They told us to come here and wait for them. So we are waiting till they come,' the eldest girl replied.

'Yes. We are waiting till our people come for us,' said all the others in chorus.

'But,' said Frau Ebermann very patiently – 'but now tell me, for I tell you that I am not in the least angry, where do you come from? Where do you come from?'

The five gave the names of two villages of which she had read in the papers.

'That is silly,' said Frau Ebermann. 'The people

fired on us, and they were punished. Those places are wiped out, stamped flat.'

'Yes, yes, wiped out, stamped flat. That is why and – I have lost the ribbon off my pigtail,' said the younger girl. She looked behind her over the sofa-back.

'It is not here,' said the elder. 'It was lost before. Don't you remember?'

'Now, if you are lost, you must go and tell our police. They will take care of you and give you food,' said Frau Ebermann. 'Anna will show you the way there.'

'No,' – this was the six-year-old with the smile, – 'we must wait here till our people come for us. Mustn't we, sister?'

'Of course. We wait here till our people come for us. All the world knows that,' said the eldest girl.

'Yes.' The boy in her lap had waked again. 'Little children, too – as little as Henri, and *he* doesn't wear trousers yet. As little as all that.'

'I don't understand,' said Frau Ebermann, shivering. In spite of the heat of the room and the damp breath of the steam-inhaler, the aspirin was not doing its duty.

The girl raised her blue eyes and looked at the woman for an instant.

'You see,' she said, emphasising her statements with her fingers, '*they* told *us* to wait *here* till *our* people came for us. So we came. We wait till our people come for us.'

'That is silly again,' said Frau Ebermann. 'It is no good for you to wait here. Do you know what this place is? You have been to school? It is Berlin, the capital of Germany.'

'Yes, yes,' they all cried; 'Berlin, capital of Germany. We know that. That is why we came.'

'So, you see, it is no good,' she said triumphantly, 'because your people can never come for you here.'

'They told us to come here and wait till our people came for us.' They delivered this as if it were a lesson in school. Then they sat still, their hands orderly folded on their laps, smiling as sweetly as ever.

'Go away! Go away!' Frau Ebermann shrieked.

'You called?' said Anna, entering.

'No. Go away! Go away!'

'Very good, old cat,' said the maid under her breath. 'Next time you *may* call,' and she returned to her friend in the kitchen.

'I ask you – ask you, *please* to go away,' Frau Ebermann pleaded. 'Go to my Anna through that door, and she will give you cakes and sweeties. It is not kind of you to come into my room and behave so badly.'

'Where else shall we go now?' the elder girl demanded, turning to her little company. They fell into discussion. One preferred the broad street with trees, another the railway station; but when she suggested an Emperor's palace, they agreed with her.

'We will go then,' she said, and added half apologetically to Frau Ebermann, 'You see, they are so little they like to meet all the others.'

'What others?' said Frau Ebermann.

'The others – hundreds and hundreds and thousands and thousands of the others.'

'That is a lie. There cannot be a hundred even, much less a thousand,' cried Frau Ebermann.

'So?' said the girl politely.

'Yes. *I* tell you; and I have very good information. I know how it happened. You should have been more careful. You should not have run out to see the horses and guns passing. That is how it is done when our troops pass through. My son has written me so.'

They had clambered down from the sofa, and gathered round the bed with eager, interested eyes.

'Horses and guns going by – how fine!' someone whispered.

'Yes, yes; believe me, *that* is how the accidents to the children happen. You must know yourself that it is true. One runs out to look – '

'But I never saw any at all,' a boy cried sorrowfully. 'Only one noise I heard. That was when Aunt Emmeline's house fell down.'

'But listen to me. *I* am telling you! One runs out to

look, because one is little and cannot see well. So one peeps between the man's legs, and then – you know how close those big horses and guns turn the corners – then one's foot slips and one gets run over. That's how it happens. Several times it had happened, but not many times; certainly not a hundred, perhaps not twenty. So, you see, you *must* be all. Tell me now that you are all that there are, and Anna shall give you the cakes.'

'Thousands,' a boy repeated monotonously. 'Then we all come here to wait till our people come for us.'

'But now we will go away from here. The poor lady is tired,' said the elder girl, plucking his sleeve.

'Oh, you hurt, you hurt!' he cried, and burst into tears.

'What is that for?' said Frau Ebermann. 'To cry in a room where a poor lady is sick is very inconsiderate.'

'Oh, but look, lady!' said the elder girl.

Frau Ebermann looked and saw.

'*Au revoir*, lady.' They made their little smiling bows and curtseys undisturbed by her loud cries. '*Au revoir*, lady. We will wait till our people come for us.'

When Anna at last ran in, she found her mistress on her knees, busily cleaning the floor with the lace cover from the radiator, because, she explained, it was all spotted with the blood of five children – she was perfectly certain there could not be more than five in the whole world – who had gone away for the moment, but were now waiting round the corner, and Anna was to find them and give them cakes to stop the bleeding, while her mistress swept and garnished that Our dear Lord when He came might find everything as it should be.

# THE CHARGE OF THE LIGHT BRIGADE

Alfred Lord Tennyson

This poem was written a few weeks after the battle it describes, in which a British brigade of light cavalry was sent to attack some retreating troops during the Crimean War in 1854. However, the order was badly communicated and instead the cavalry found themselves charging at a heavily defended enemy line. While future war poets would focus on the mistakes made by senior officers, this poem focuses on the valour of the soldiers, nobly following orders even though it is obviously a hopeless mission.

# THE CHARGE OF THE LIGHT BRIGADE

## Alfred Lord Tennyson

### I

Half a league, half a league,
Half a league onward,
All in the valley of Death
   Rode the six hundred.
'Forward, the Light Brigade!
Charge for the guns!' he said.
Into the valley of Death
   Rode the six hundred.

### II

'Forward, the Light Brigade!'
Was there a man dismayed?
Not though the soldier knew
   Someone had blundered.
Theirs not to make reply,
Theirs not to reason why,

Theirs but to do and die.
Into the valley of Death
   Rode the six hundred.

## III

Cannon to right of them,
Cannon to left of them,
Cannon in front of them
   Volleyed and thundered;
Stormed at with shot and shell,
Boldly they rode and well,
Into the jaws of Death,
Into the mouth of hell
   Rode the six hundred.

## IV

Flashed all their sabres bare,
Flashed as they turned in air
Sabring the gunners there,
Charging an army, while
   All the world wondered.
Plunged in the battery-smoke
Right through the line they broke;
Cossack and Russian
Reeled from the sabre stroke
   Shattered and sundered.

Then they rode back, but not
    Not the six hundred.

## V

Cannon to right of them,
Cannon to left of them,
Cannon behind them
    Volleyed and thundered;
Stormed at with shot and shell,
While horse and hero fell.
They that had fought so well
Came through the jaws of Death,
Back from the mouth of hell,
All that was left of them,
    Left of six hundred.

## VI

When can their glory fade?
O the wild charge they made!
    All the world wondered.
Honour the charge they made!
Honour the Light Brigade,
    Noble six hundred!

# DULCE ET DECORUM EST

## Wilfred Owen

This is possibly the best-known anti-war poem in the English language. Written during the First World War by a young man with personal experience of the horrors of trench warfare, the poem was a bitter response to the attitudes of any who did not fight but encouraged young men to enlist. *Dulce et decorum est pro patria mori* is a Latin quote from the poet Horace that would have been well known at the time as it was often quoted in war propaganda. It translates as *How sweet and right it is to die for one's country.*

# DULCE ET DECORUM EST

## Wilfred Owen

Bent double, like old beggars under sacks,
Knock-kneed, coughing like hags, we cursed through sludge,
Till on the haunting flares we turned our backs
And towards our distant rest began to trudge.
Men marched asleep. Many had lost their boots
But limped on, blood-shod. All went lame; all blind;
Drunk with fatigue; deaf even to the hoots
Of tired, outstripped Five-Nines that dropped behind.
Gas! Gas! Quick, boys! – An ecstasy of fumbling,
Fitting the clumsy helmets just in time;
But someone still was yelling out and stumbling,
And flound'ring like a man in fire or lime ...
Dim, through the misty panes and thick green light,
As under a green sea, I saw him drowning.
In all my dreams, before my helpless sight,
He plunges at me, guttering, choking, drowning.
If in some smothering dreams you too could pace

Behind the wagon that we flung him in,
And watch the white eyes writhing in his face,
His hanging face, like a devil's sick of sin;
If you could hear, at every jolt, the blood
Come gargling from the froth-corrupted lungs,
Obscene as cancer, bitter as the cud
Of vile, incurable sores on innocent tongues,
My friend, you would not tell with such high zest
To children ardent for some desperate glory,
The old Lie; Dulce et Decorum est
Pro patria mori.

# TOMMY
## Rudyard Kipling

A Tommy – a redcoat, a British soldier – speaks to us bitterly about the two-faced people back home who give returning soldiers a hard time. Quick to complain about squaddies and their rough behaviour, they are even quicker to cheer them on and hide behind them at the first sign of attack. Rudyard Kipling was a staunch supporter of British soldiers and believed that they were let down by public perception at home, as well as by the incompetence of politicians.

# TOMMY

## Rudyard Kipling

I went into a public 'ouse to get a pint o' beer,
The publican 'e up an' sez, 'We serve no red-coats here.'
The girls be'ind the bar they laughed an' giggled fit to die,
I outs into the street again an' to myself sez I:
O it's Tommy this, an' Tommy that, an' 'Tommy, go away';
But it's 'Thank you, Mister Atkins', when the band begins to play
The band begins to play, my boys, the band begins to play,
O it's 'Thank you, Mister Atkins', when the band begins to play.

I went into a theatre as sober as could be,
They gave a drunk civilian room, but 'adn't none for me;
They sent me to the gallery or round the music-'alls,

But when it comes to fightin', Lord! they'll shove me
in the stalls!
For it's Tommy this, an' Tommy that, an' 'Tommy,
wait outside';
But it's 'Special train for Atkins', when the trooper's
on the tide
The troopship's on the tide, my boys, the troopship's
on the tide,
O it's 'Special train for Atkins', when the trooper's on
the tide.

Yes, makin' mock o' uniforms that guard you while
you sleep
Is cheaper than them uniforms, an' they're
starvation cheap.
An' hustlin' drunken soldiers when they're goin'
large a bit
Is five times better business than paradin' in full kit.
Then it's Tommy this, an' Tommy that, an' 'Tommy,
'ow's yer soul?'
But it's 'Thin red line of 'eroes', when the drums
begin to roll
The drums begin to roll, my boys, the drums begin
to roll,
O it's 'Thin red line of 'eroes', when the drums begin
to roll.

We aren't no thin red 'eroes, nor we aren't no blackguards too,
But single men in barricks, most remarkable like you;
An' if sometimes our conduck isn't all your fancy paints,
Why, single men in barricks don't grow into plaster saints;
While it's Tommy this, an' Tommy that, an' 'Tommy, fall be'ind',
But it's 'Please to walk in front, sir', when there's trouble in the wind
There's trouble in the wind, my boys, there's trouble in the wind,
O it's 'Please to walk in front, sir', when there's trouble in the wind.

You talk o' better food for us, an' schools, an' fires, an' all:
We'll wait for extry rations if you treat us rational.
Don't mess about the cook-room slops, but prove it to our face
The Widow's Uniform is not the soldier-man's disgrace.
For it's Tommy this, an' Tommy that, an' 'Chuck him out, the brute!'
But it's 'Saviour of 'is country', when the guns begin to shoot;

An' it's Tommy this, an' Tommy that, an' anything you please;
An' Tommy ain't a bloomin' fool – you bet that Tommy sees!

# IN TIMES OF PEACE

## John Agard

John Agard's poem, written in 2009 as the war in Afghanistan continued on and on, explores the challenge of coming home from war. We are more culturally aware than ever of some of the psychological problems returning soldiers face. 'In Times of Peace' includes imagery of striking contrasts – bubble bath and bodies, boots and butterflies – all designed to help us as readers, who have never been to war, to try to imagine the unimaginable.

# IN TIMES OF PEACE

## John Agard

That finger – index to be exact –
so used to a trigger's warmth
how will it begin to deal with skin
that threatens only to embrace?

Those feet, so at home in heavy boots
and stepping over bodies –
how will they cope with a bubble bath
when foam is all there is for ambush?

And what of hearts in times of peace?
Will war-worn hearts grow sluggish
like Valentine roses wilting
without the adrenalin of a bullet's blood-rush?

When the dust of peace has settled on a nation,
how will human arms handle the death of weapons?
And what of ears, are ears so tuned to sirens
that the closing of wings causes a tremor?

As for eyes, are eyes ready for the soft dance
of a butterfly's bootless invasion?